OPENING
THE KIMONO

I honor you !
Blessings,
Theresa

PRAISE FOR *OPENING THE KIMONO*

"Reading *Opening the Kimono* was like coming up for air after an aimless swim in a lifelong emotional pool. This book is CPR for the psyche. In mere chapters, author Theresa Rose breaks down complex issues that might have taken other writers volumes (and loads of esoteric mumbo-jumbo) to even begin to explore. Just as Betty Friedan tackled the "problem that has no name" in *The Feminine Mystique*, Rose offers a women's Bible that is as groundbreaking for the new millennium as Friedan's was for the '60s.

Rose helps debunk these centuries of programming that have left women unsure of who they are and uncomfortable with accepting who they might truly be. She asks why and she offers substantial why not's. Her sense of humor and humility set her apart from the dime-a-dozen holier than thou spiritual authors that make it sound so easy when it's really so damn hard.

I needed this book. I needed to view myself in this book. I needed to relive my life through this book. I saw my own missteps in Rose's experiences that were conveyed with such a raw, funny and universal spirit. I never felt like a saint on a cloud was talking down to me. I felt like I was right in Rose's arms the entire time.

After thousands of dollars spent on psychiatry sessions and perfect outfits that I thought time and time again might finally do the trick, I am so grateful to have stumbled upon this book. Let the dominoes start falling."

—ABBY WEINGARTEN,
Features Correspondent, *Sarasota Herald-Tribune*

"This book is truly a gift that keeps giving. As I moved from page to page with great anticipation, I felt as if I was given vignettes of Theresa's life and the gems she trusted to share with her readers. I uncovered a part of myself as I opened to her story.

The magic of a life lived without hiding takes great courage and commitment to be conscious and awake. Without judging her choices made in the past, Theresa gives us all permission to remember that the most spiritual act of all is self-acceptance. Thank you, Theresa Rose, for allowing the fragrance of your open heart to sweetly inspire and touch my life and many who will open the pages of this beautiful book."

—FRANNIE HOFFMAN,
author of *From Modeling Clothes to Modeling Self*

"This book opens not only a kimono, but a potent lens to the female psyche going through climate change in the home, the world, and beyond. In these pages, men will finally understand women, and women will come to understand our trials, tribulations, and triumphs in the poignant truths of everyday life. Theresa Rose outs us all."

ANODEA JUDITH,
author of *Wheels of Life, Waking the Global Heart*

"*Opening the Kimono* is simply amazing. This book has made me laugh, cry and simply look at myself and my own life in a much more honest and less critical fashion. It is funny without being sarcastic, honest and literal without being intrusive, and spiritually guiding without being preachy.

In short, it is simply word-crack. Once you have had some, you have to have more and if you try to put it down, *Opening the Kimono* just calls you back to her like some erotically seductive entity that you just can't resist. Yeah—word-crack.

Kudos to Theresa Rose for bringing this masterpiece into the world."

—SONIE LASKER,
author and freelance journalist

OPENING
THE KIMONO

A Woman's Intimate Journey
Through Life's Biggest Challenges

THERESA ROSE

ISBN-13: 978-0-9818869-0-9
ISBN-10: 0-9818869-0-6

Library of Congress Cataloging-in-Publication Data

Rose, Theresa
    Opening the Kimono : a woman's intimate journey through life's biggest challenges / Theresa Rose.
    —1st ed.
    p. cm.
    LCCN   2008906697
    ISBN-13 978-0-9818869-0-9
    ISBN-10 0-9818869-0-6
    1. Body, Mind & Spirit/Inspiration & Personal Growth. 2. Self-Help/Motivational & Inspirational. 3. Biography & Autobiography/Personal Memoirs.

For more information on the author's work, visit www.theresarose.net

Cover photography: www.wayneeastep.com
Author photography: www.stephaniedubskyphotography.com
Cover design: www.jackdavis.com
Interior book design: John Reinhardt Book Design, www.bookdesign.com

Printed and bound in the United States of America.

To my beloved mother Kaylene Hansen,
whose graceful, courageous, and conscious transition
into the Spirit World inspired me to find my voice.

CONTENTS

❧

INTRODUCTION

Becoming an Emotional Exhibitionist   3

MY BODY

True Confessions   9
Getting to Know My Body   12
An Epiphany in the Target Dressing Room   16
Choosing Carrots Over Chee-tos   19
Dancing Queen   24
Therapy For My Colon   27
The Anatomy of a Binge   30
It's Only a Number   35
The Face of the Devil   40
Coming Out of the Smoke-Filled Closet   44

LOVE & SEX

The Unsexy Side of Sex   53
I Chased Him 'Til He Caught Me   57
The Curse of Having a Hottie for a Husband   63

ix

To Vibe or Not to Vibe 66
In Defense of Scheduling Sex 69
Taming the Beast 73
Choices Have Consequences 76

RAISING KIDS

Fetal Wisdom 83
Having a Baby: No Assembly Required 87
The Siren's Call of Pacifiers, TV and EasyMac 90
Slaying the Bogeyman 94
Because I Said So 98
Growing Pains 102
Diary of a Mad First Grader 105
My Greatest Teacher 108

CAREER

It Isn't About the Pink Stuff 113
I Am Not My Title 117
From the Boardroom to the Treatment Room 121
Beauty or the Beast 126
No Time Off for Good Behavior 130
Failing Forward 133

DEATH

The Conversation on the Couch 141
Death Through the Eyes of a Child 146
A Painful Reminder 149
The Right Words at the Right Time 153
Music To Cry To 156
The High Heel and the Cardinal 159
Never Forget From Whence You Came 162
The Year of Firsts 166

CONTENTS

LIBERATION

A Rose By Any Other Name   171
Embracing What Is   175
Calgon, Take Me Away!   179
Victimgirl   182
Finding God in the Dining Room   187
Opening Your Own Kimono   191

Club Kimono Discussion Starters   195
Acknowledgments   203
About the Author   206

INTRODUCTION

"Life is an opportunity, benefit from it ~
Life is a beauty, admire it ~ Life is a dream, realize it ~
Life is a challenge, meet it ~ Life is a duty, complete it ~
Life is a game, play it ~ Life is a promise, fulfill it
Life is sorrow, overcome it ~ Life is a song, sing it ~
Life is a struggle, accept it ~ Life is a tragedy, confront it ~
Life is an adventure, dare it ~ Life is luck, make it ~
Life is life, fight for it!"

—MOTHER TERESA

Becoming an Emotional Exhibitionist

HOW IS IT THAT SOME PEOPLE have picture-perfect lives in which they maintain fabulous figures, manage successful careers, have perpetually clean houses, take romantic getaways with their gorgeous spouses, lead the parents volunteer program at school, create charming scrapbooks for their children, and always have that blinding smile plastered on their pimple-free, wrinkle-free faces? Please tell me I am not the only one who wonders what sort of contract with the devil these rare freaks of nature have signed.

The truth is that no one is without flaws, regardless of how it looks to the casual observer. Every one of us has secrets, scars, and skeletons. As an energy healer and meditation facilitator, I have worked with hundreds of people who have a great recipe and all the right ingredients for a fulfilling life, but who consistently don't like what comes out of the oven. Their joy is muted, and they often struggle to find meaning among the clamor of jobs, relationships, domestic responsibilities, and other obligations. They *want* to be happy, but they're not.

I know so well how they feel because I have walked the same path. On the surface, it would seem that I have my act together. I am a happily married woman and mother of the most fabulous first grader on the planet. I earn a living as an alternative healer, meditation guide, and motivational speaker, helping people discover their own relationship with the Divine. For the most part I'm a happy camper. But that's just one side of me.

Like nearly everyone else, there is a hidden side to me. To the outside world I am a grounded, confident woman, but in my private moments, I sometimes morph into a raving lunatic riddled with insecurities. How is it that I can be a dynamic woman one moment and a Little Miss SuperWuss the next? Because I *am* both of those people. Some days I am in the groove: feeling great, creating the day as I desire, trusting that all is well, and experiencing life as a blissful romp. Then there are days when I become easily distracted, struggle against every little obstacle, and get paralyzed by fear. At this point my goal is to be a powerful, spiritual beacon as often as possible and minimize (dare I say eliminate?!) time spent as a powerless, whiny weenie.

Opening the Kimono is a tell-all, diary, rant, confession, and healing guide all rolled into one. Writing it was like going to therapy each and every day. I describe how my life isn't always fun, how I sometimes make terrible choices, how insecure I can be, and how I work to heal old childhood wounds. I also share how life is a glorious gift filled with amazing opportunities for happiness, growth and recovery despite the challenges it sometimes brings.

I think we all wear kimonos of some kind. A kimono is an exquisitely adorned, multi-layered garment that completely covers one's nakedness, one's essence. Similarly, we wrap ourselves tightly in layers of propriety, calculation and protection, never allowing anyone to see us at our most vulnerable. By doing so, we insulate our fragile interior while presenting an appealing, socially acceptable exterior for the judging eyes of the outside world. *Opening the Kimono* is about exposing our soft underbellies and the power that comes from that act of courage. Through opening my kimono I have become healthier, more present, and best of all, more joyful than I ever dreamed possible.

By baring my gunk for all to see I have freed myself from its chokehold. I reveal secrets I've kept from family and friends for decades and dig into deeply buried emotional traumas. My stories, raw and intimate, give a private glimpse of my innermost thoughts and feelings regarding my mother's illness and death, marriage and sex, parenting, addiction, career ups and downs, and a lifelong battle with weight.

You will read all sorts of icky stuff, every bit of which was terrifying to put down on paper. In fact, I made a promise to myself I would not write anything that didn't scare the crap out of me. In the process, I learned that diving into the scary stuff wasn't so bad after all. On the contrary, life got juicier when I walked through the fire to conquer my biggest demons. Living and speaking the truth were therapeutic, empowering and liberating even though it terrified me and sometimes made me seem like a crazy person.

Over the years I have undergone major transformations and experienced dramatic shifts in consciousness through awareness, honesty, faith, and good old-fashioned guts. I have gotten closer to Spirit as I know It and have made some fairly decent choices. Hopefully I will show that one can be deeply spiritual while being irreverent, sassy, sexy, and sometimes downright crass.

Make no mistake; I am not professing to know all there is about living the perfect life. In fact, it often seems I have more breakdowns than breakthroughs. As you read my stories and the lessons learned, I give you full permission to take what I say as complete bunk. I'm very confident in my belief system and have no problem with someone thinking I don't know what the heck I'm talking about.

Having always encouraged my students and clients to practice discernment, I now suggest the same for you. Run everything through your own filter and take only those lessons with which you resonate. Read each chapter like you are going through the racks at your favorite department store. Find the gems you love and take them with you; leave those that don't quite fit your belief, style, body or budget. I trust you will find a few nuggets to assist you on your journey toward a happier, healthier, and more meaningful life.

It is my fervent wish that while reading my tale, you recognize your own experiences and find inspiration, comfort, and guidance as you walk your personal path. At its core, *Opening the Kimono* is a celebration of life, affirming that each of us is a spiritual being destined to revel in joy, beauty and love. This isn't a dress rehearsal, baby, so let's get out there and start living juicy!

MY BODY

"The ultimate lesson all of us have to learn
is unconditional love, which includes not only others
but ourselves as well."

—Elizabeth Kübler-Ross

TRUE CONFESSIONS

I AM OVERWEIGHT. There. I said it. It's out in the open and I'll no longer be powerless over that statement.

I have been heavy my whole life. Somewhere around six years of age my adorable baby fat just became fat. Buried in my deepest, darkest corners are painful memories of other children ridiculing me because of my weight. As a result, I grew up being ashamed of my body. To add insult to injury, I was one of the first girls in my class to get her period and develop breasts. Yay! What a joy it was to be cruelly picked on by a mob of twelve-year olds in the girls' bathroom. I firmly believe nearly every girl in the sixth grade is temporarily abducted and replaced with an evil, alien twit.

At thirteen I went on my first diet: Weight Watchers. My mother drove me to the meetings, and I remember quietly surveying all of the "old" (read my current age) fat women desperately wanting to lose weight, be thin, be seen, be appreciated, and be beautiful. I realize that I am now one of those women that the young me was so frightened of becoming.

Diets have been a part of my life forever. You name it, I've been on it. I've lost hundreds of pounds over the years, and every moment of it sucked. My moods would be at the mercy of the scale. If I lost weight that week (.25 pounds!), I'd be ecstatic. If I maintained my weight or, God forbid, *gained*, I would be devastated. Exercise was always recommended as a part of the weight loss regimen, and I hated every last minute of it; working-out was a horror from start to finish. The foods I had to consume weren't any better. Just the thought of ingesting one more #^@king rice cake sends chills down my spine.

Because of our culture's fanatical focus on beauty I would force myself to continue the torture. Everywhere I went I saw skinny, beautiful girls being admired, having fun, and getting the guys. I wanted to be one of them; I wanted the size 4 Calvin Klein jeans and the hot boyfriend! I craved the love they seemed to effortlessly receive. Thanks to my deprivation and dedication, the weight would start to come off. People would notice me more, and I would begin to attract the much-sought-after attention from the opposite sex! Woo hoo!

But there was always a point where the attention got to be uncomfortable. The wrong guy would show too much interest and something bad would happen—mostly small stuff but some big stuff too—causing me to feel unsafe in the world...again. Unable to cope with my fears, I would instinctively go on a binge, finding food deliciously anesthetizing. At the end of the week I would have naturally regained some of the lost weight. Depressed due to my increased poundage, I'd fall deeper into the abyss of binge-eating, causing an even greater backslide. After a few weeks, the guilt of failing yet again became so debilitating that I'd return to unconsciously stuffing myself and growing roots on the couch. This self-destructive cycle repeated itself for years.

In order to fit in socially, I compensated for my larger-than-average girth with my intellect, wit, and growing willingness to defile myself sexually. I lived my life in my head, and my body became the enemy. Bathed in self-loathing, I avoided mirrors, cameras, clothing stores, swimming pools, and sex with the lights on. Yet I couldn't bring myself to admit that I was overweight, unhealthy, and disconnected from my body.

Seeing my fortieth birthday looming ever-nearer on the horizon, I was finally ready to dive into The Big Issue for the last time. My first step in the healing process was to seek the help of a skilled therapist to help me understand what emotional nasties lurked underneath my flab. The work we did together provided me with invaluable clarity on the deeper meaning behind my body issues. I am starting to understand the reasons *why* I chose an overweight body in the first place. By sinking into the root causes of my food addiction, I was ultimately able to identify healthier ways to meet my emotional needs. Slowly but surely I am learning that I neither want nor need to hold on to my fat to feel safe, grounded, and present.

This time around I'm asking for lots of help. I am graciously accepting assistance from my husband, daughter, friends, teachers, healers, and most importantly, Spirit. I know I have allowed this issue to be bigger than I am for nearly my entire life; I also know I can and will choose a different outcome. If you include yourself in the majority of people who hate some (or all) of their bodies, I invite you to join me on this journey. Through honesty, courage and a connection to the Divine, we can face our biggest internal demons and emerge victorious. Won't it feel great to finally get to a point where we truly and unconditionally *love* ourselves?

GETTING TO KNOW MY BODY

I AM OCCUPYING scary new territory: my body. Despite having a professional background in massage therapy, meditation, and energy healing, I have never truly been *in* my body. I was like a giant head, thinking my way through life instead of feeling it. Now, as I begin to consciously address my body acceptance and weight issues, I am starting to notice how I actually feel. And you know what? Right now I feel like crap.

As part of my latest focus on health I am regularly practicing yoga and going to the gym. At first I approached my workouts in the usual way—with utter dread. My thoughts were consumed by identifying the minimum activity levels in duration and frequency, optimal calories burned, and other analytical facets of any hyper-obsessive exercise program. However, my fixations were not solely limited to exercise. I also spent a fair amount of time fearing what others would think of me in stretchy workout clothes when I exposed my jiggles for all to see. Clearly I was still firmly in my head even while moving my body.

Despite my mental masturbation, I pressed on with the workouts. The other day I stepped up the physical challenge and attended my first Caribbean dance class. It kicked my ass up one side and down the other. Ana, the unbelievably gorgeous Peruvian Goddess/dance instructor, shook her perfect booty like a Las Vegas showgirl. Throughout the one hour sweat-a-thon I watched her jaw-dropping moves, desperately trying to copy them while not appearing like one in the throes of a grand mal seizure. Not only was it physically impossible to keep up with the lightning-fast steps of the dance diva, the ordeal was starting to inflict major damage to my already-bruised self-esteem.

As I flailed around the dance floor never quite getting in sync with Ana's sensual movements, I caught a peek at myself in the mirror and glanced back at the South American Goddess. Ana wore a white workout bra, skin-tight red pants, and an orange belly dancing coin belt; I wore a boxy t-shirt, baggy black workout pants, and gym shoes. Ana glistened; I sweated like a pig. Ana was the epitome of sex appeal; I felt like a pimply, uncoordinated junior high schooler at her first dance. At the end of the grueling hour I was definitely *in* my body, my t-shirt was drenched, and I was 99% sure I burned off the pepperoni pizza I ate over the weekend. Even so, I decided that attending any future Caribbean dance classes with Ana would be too brutally masochistic, even for me.

I have always viewed exercise as grueling punishment and would do it only under extreme internal duress. If I was going to truly fall in love with my physical self, this old way of thinking needed to change. A radical attitude adjustment was called for. From that point forward, I stopped using the word 'exercise'; it would now be known as movement. No longer would I angrily slog through the experience or be consumed by academic details of my weekly workouts. Instead I was determined to move my body how and when it wanted—with awareness, freedom, and joy.

With this in mind I modified my yoga practice, choosing only those postures I wanted and needed instead of following my usual sequence. Moving in super-slow motion and breathing deeply into every nook and cranny brought to the surface the uncomfortable sensations in my muscles and joints. With eyes closed, I sunk into each posture thinking only of how each pose made me feel. I was curious to see how my body would respond to this increased awareness. And respond it did. It yelled, "Tight! Restricted! Crunchy! Repressed! Tender! Weak!" Shaken yet undeterred, I continued to let these uncensored feelings emerge. Honestly acknowledging the blocks within me was essential in understanding what parts required deeper healing.

Getting into my body also meant becoming more cognizant of my posture. I realized I habitually sucked in my stomach, tilted my pelvis backward, and slouched my shoulders in an effort to minimize my bulging abdomen. Pa-lease. Who was I kidding? My contortions didn't hide my belly rolls and only served to create chronic lower back issues. To correct my bad habit I gradually retrained myself to stand more erect and in proper alignment. Ouch! The pain of releasing my tight abdominal and back muscles, aligning my spine, and unlocking my pelvis had me fully appreciating how harmful it was to lug around fifty or more extra pounds all these years.

So often had I categorically denied physical discomfort that actually *feeling* these sensations was nearly overwhelming. Self-recrimination flooded me as I cradled my protruding gut and angrily berated myself for being fat. Eventually I stopped the mental beatings and took note of how easy it was to fall back into the well-established pattern of self-hate.

It was glaringly obvious that my belly was my biggest nemesis. If I wanted to stop loathing my midsection I needed to recognize it as more than my squishy part I avoided at all costs. Instead it needed to be seen as the physical result of a lifetime of choices. My big round belly existed because I chose to distrust my body, allowed food to soothe emotional wounds, and let the beliefs of others be more important than my own.

Because I've been in physical disharmony for so long, I had a hard time perceiving myself as a healthy, vibrant being. It was almost impossible to look in the mirror without judging what I saw. Considering I had spent nearly a lifetime hating my reflection, I knew it would take a while to break the long-standing habit of self-judgment. Calling on Spirit for support, I committed to making courageous new choices as often as possible. I would do my best to start loving myself, eating consciously, tackling my dramas and traumas head-on, and being guided by my own beliefs rather than those of others.

Jean, my best friend in the world, recently gave me some brilliant advice. She wisely said, "Imagine each extra pound you carry as a pound of emotion." Thanks to Jean's words of wisdom, I now hold my big belly with tenderness and love, honoring it as a part of my history. I unconsciously created this extra weight to serve me over the years, and I can just as easily (OK, maybe not *just* as easily) release it when I so choose.

With each passing day it is getting easier to move my body. I am feeling a little better, I am less self-conscious, and most importantly, I am happier. My furtive glimpses in the mirror are becoming more frequent and less hate-filled. In fact, on rare occasions, I have even gone so far as to acknowledge the gorgeous woman with killer curves that stares back at me. To be sure, this budding relationship with myself is developing slowly and sometimes painfully, but I am finally learning to accept, embrace and love my jiggles instead of curse them.

An Epiphany in the Target Dressing Room

THE OTHER DAY a woman inadvertently flashed me in the Target fitting room. No, she didn't accidentally reveal her private parts while trying on the latest swimsuits. Her indecent exposure was of something far more personal: her insecurities.

Most of us have been systematically brainwashed into thinking that we simply aren't good enough as we are. Tabloid magazines barrage us with a double whammy, taunting us with airbrushed glossies of the fifty most beautiful people in the world while simultaneously blasting us with unflattering photos of celebrities and their cellulite, protruding bellies, wrinkles, and other human "flaws". One brief glance at these periodicals while in the supermarket checkout line can leave me feeling like Quasimodo by the time I swipe my debit card.

We have been thoroughly convinced we are the embodiment of failure because some advertisement, article, TV show, or movie tells us we don't have the right look, clothes, body, or life. By constantly comparing ourselves to these fantasies, our inner critics label us as too fat, thin, flat-chested, big-breasted, ugly, short, tall, or defective in some other way. How else can you explain why high school girls across the country are asking for and receiving plastic surgery as graduation gifts?

Given my history of body acceptance issues as well the hyper-critical social climate in which we live, it is challenging for me to be in my body and love it regardless of its size. I've been using the Law of Attraction to traverse these murky waters of the ego. This universal law suggests that, in order for us to manifest our dreams, we need to stay in a positive emotional state as much as possible, focusing on what we want rather than what we *don't* want. A popular phrase that captures the essence of the Law of Attraction is "what we think about we bring about."

I recently decided to employ the Law of Attraction during an excursion to Target. Historically, shopping for clothes has been a horror show where nearly every item I choose either doesn't fit right or looks atrocious on me. How heartbreaking it is to find the perfect, super-cute outfit to wear at some important shindig only to find that I *literally* can't get my butt into it. This type of wardrobe malfunction has happened to me numerous times, causing me to wallow in self-pity for days afterward.

On this particular day of despair I slowly waded through the racks to pick out the few items that a) were in my size, b) were reasonably appropriate for a 37-year old woman to wear, and c) didn't make me look like a house. After several pass-throughs I settled on a few safe items and entered Satan's Dressing Room complete with triple full-length mirrors and the oh-so-flattering florescent lights. During the zip-up process I began to mutter, "I love myself...I'm beautiful just as I am...I'm joyous as I try on these new clothes." As I earnestly repeated my mantras, there was a part of me that actually believed what I was saying! That's real growth.

At the same time another woman about my age entered the dressing room with her mother. As the daughter tried on her selected items she bitterly complained about how awful she looked. Her voice was rife with self-hatred as she repeatedly referred to herself as "disgusting" and a "fat pig", telling her mother that fat girls can't wear the kinds of clothes she chose. She announced that she absolutely *had* to go on a diet right away and continued her self-abusive rant for several minutes. Shockingly, her mother quietly and ever-so-politely *agreed with her daughter*. I was horrified as I listened to this woman verbally flagellate herself with her mother in full support. Moments later the daughter said, "Last year I was a size 4 and now I'm a bulging size 8!" Whoa...hold the phone! This chick was a size 8 and she's freaking out about being fat?! If she's a fat pig at a size 8, I couldn't even fathom what my size 16 made me.

Just then it hit me. Like so many of us, this woman had been manipulated by a society that worships thin and degrades thick, broadcasts television programs about extreme makeovers and big losers, and conditions us to believe that a size 4 is normal and a size 8 is disgusting. The media, pop culture, and, worst of all, her mother taught her to value what's on the outside more than what's on the inside. Sadly, she bought into The Lie—hook, line and sinker.

As a quiet witness to this stranger's growing shame I began to feel great compassion for her. It became painfully clear that she was totally unplugged from her personal power and didn't recognize her own intrinsic beauty. I silently said a prayer to Spirit that someday soon this woman would wake up from her media-induced haze, realize the Divine perfection that she was, and start to love herself unconditionally. Then I slowly turned toward the full-length mirrors, stared unflinchingly at my reflection, and solemnly said the same prayer for myself.

Choosing Carrots
Over Chee-tos

MOST OF MY CHILDHOOD MEALS came from a box, a bag or a waiter. I am from the processed foods generation and was raised by my hard-working, tough-but-tender mother. My mom made it perfectly clear that she was disinterested in all things culinary and had no desire to ingest food that was healthy and nutritious. Since Mom was a size 2 waif weighing in at one hundred pounds soaking wet, she thought she never needed to be concerned with proper diet. (Her body was one that women would strive to emulate and over which men would salivate.) To her, food was a necessary evil and she expended as little energy as possible preparing it.

Cost, convenience and taste were the sole deciding factors when it came to mealtime; Stouffer's TV dinners, Swanson's chicken pot pies and Kraft's macaroni and cheese were popular favorites. A steady diet of these processed foods along with other fat-laden accompaniments resulted in one of life's cruel injustices: a perpetually stick-thin mother and her ever-expanding chubby daughter.

I can't say that my childhood was totally exempt of fruits and vegetables. Sometimes we had bananas, raisins, and the rare orange in the kitchen. With these few exceptions, Mom saw fruit as either too expensive or too much hassle. On the vegetable front we ate mostly frozen green beans or broccoli and cauliflower smothered in cheese sauce. (Mom would always try to convince me that eating mashed potatoes constituted a serving of vegetables.) Our protein offerings were usually beef, pork or chicken with precious little seafood gracing our table.

To save time my mother also took me out to eat a lot. From a very young age I was a master at deciphering menus, identifying the tastiest—and often the unhealthiest—choice from each course. I became well-versed in the yummy world of appetizers, the best-tasting pasta sauces (Alfredo!), and which desserts were flambéed. My typical dinner order at the neighborhood Country Kitchen was a grilled cheese sandwich, french fries, a Coke and chocolate pudding. No wonder I went to Weight Watchers at thirteen.

Please don't misunderstand. I am not for a moment blaming my mother for my lifelong struggle with weight. She was clearly doing her best with what she perceived as a limited amount of time, money and energy. Moreover, Mom's mealtime choices reflected her rural Midwest upbringing; she was raised on meat and potatoes, not salmon and steamed veggies. During a recent trip to her tiny hometown, my husband and I went to the one and only restaurant for lunch. The tiny café had a huge menu with upwards of a hundred items. Nearly every selection was fried and most were smothered in some kind of sauce or gravy. As I searched for something reasonably healthy to eat, I discovered the one item that wasn't deep-fried or gooped-up: "the Diet Plate". It consisted of a hamburger patty, a hard-boiled egg, cottage cheese, and iceberg lettuce with ranch dressing. Yum…doesn't that sound delicious? Considering this bleak dietary environment, I am not surprised that my mom didn't have a clue about enjoying nutritious foods.

When I started Weight Watchers I got my first lesson in the world of natural, unprocessed foods. The meeting leader gave me a booklet identifying the allowable foods and their proper portions. The program categorized them as fruits, vegetables, proteins, starches, fats, and extras. As I leafed through the pamphlet I felt confident I could find things to eat in the starches and extras categories; it was the other areas that were going to be problematic. Sadly I wasn't even familiar with several of the produce items on the list. (What the hell is a kumquat anyway? I still wouldn't be able to pick one out in a lineup.)

When I showed Mom the details of the diet she grumbled, "Well, I guess you'll have to eat more fruits and vegetables from now on." From that moment until just recently, I saw the consumption of produce as punishment for being fat. Rarely, if ever, did I perceive eating natural foods as a joyful experience. During that first diet and the many others that followed over the years, I begrudgingly ate the required foods like a petulant child being forced to clean her plate. I can't help but think of how much self-hatred I ingested with each bite.

My relationship with food is getting better, but it is not without its growing pains. My particular cross to bear is a nasty sugar addiction. When one has been conditioned to eat only highly-processed foods, the switch to whole foods can be jarring. Let's be honest, sugar tastes so damn good! To refuse the sweet temptress, I am trying to focus on how easily my system processes the healthy stuff and how clogged-up it gets when I eat the bad stuff. No part of my body except my taste buds wants or needs things like Reese's Peanut Butter Cups.

Because of my sketchy culinary history I'd still be chowing-down on Ho-Ho's or Taco Bell if taste were the only factor. In order to create a new relationship with food I had to look at it holistically. I am trying to appreciate food as the energy source it truly is instead of enjoying it solely for its taste. I have learned that the closer my food choices are to Mother Nature, as opposed to factories and warehouses, the more energy I receive and the less my body works to absorb it. The more vitality I receive from my food, the more efficient my organs function and the better my body looks and feels.

That's all fine and dandy in the perfect world, but the last time I checked, my zip code isn't in that world. When I get stressed-out my mind gets all foggy and I no longer see food as just sustenance. Food morphs into a delicious narcotic that reliably soothes my emotional aches and pains. When I'm upset, eating a "reasonable" portion of fresh fruits and vegetables doesn't come remotely close to satisfying me as much as shoveling a bagful of Oreo Double Stuf cookies into my mouth followed by a tall milk chaser. In fact, my love affair with these delectable black and white beauties dates back to early childhood. I frequently consumed mass quantities of them in an effort to relieve the hurt feelings from my latest wound of the heart. I can still vividly recall an elaborate covert cookie operation I orchestrated as an eight-year old. One sad afternoon I carefully stacked the sweet medicine one on top of the other from my wrist to my armpit and sneaked past my mother's watchful eye into my bedroom. I locked myself in and quickly scarfed them down in silence and shame.

How can I break this long-standing addiction? How can I navigate life's tough moments without reaching for food to comfort me like a second mother? Honestly, I don't know. I'm not sure I'll ever be totally free of these behaviors. Instead of completely ridding myself of them, I am simply trying to become aware of my emotions *before* I put anything in my mouth. It all boils down to one simple question: am I eating because my body needs energy or because I need to be nurtured?

If the answer is the latter, I ask myself what else will satisfy my need for nurturing. Maybe I need to simply unplug for a little while and do something nice for *me*. My favorite escapes are going for a walk, taking a bubble bath, having a catnap, talking on the telephone with a good friend, practicing yoga, or playing the piano. I'll go through each of my options and imagine how I'll feel after doing them. The activity that generates the warmest feeling within me is the one I choose. By trusting my gut instinct and asking my body what it *really* needs, I get back to center every time.

The problem isn't figuring out what non-eating things I can do to be good to myself, it's taking the time to actually *do* them. The concept of making my needs a priority is a foreign one. I'm so used to tuning-out how I feel that I often don't even know I'm unhappy or stressed until my husband or daughter points it out to me. Even when I realize that I am in dire need of nurturing, I struggle with valuing myself enough to pull away from the activity at hand—whether that's work, cleaning, bills, laundry, shopping, or cooking—and do those things that promote healing. This is what victimhood looks like. It sure isn't pretty.

However, when I do recognize my emotional needs and act upon them, a whole new way of being presents itself. By moving into the natural flow of life instead of pushing against the powerful current of self-destruction, the lure of binge eating diminishes. Luckily, each day affords me brand new opportunities to eat consciously rather than falling into the decades-old habit of unconscious shoveling. I am finally learning to enjoy every last bite, even if it's from the occasional Double Stuf Oreo.

DANCING QUEEN

❦

L AST WEEK I FELT LIKE I DANCED for the first time. While attending a week-long healing workshop I moved my jiggly-wiggly bod to the joyous rhythms of music without worrying about who was watching or what I looked like. Now I understand what all the fuss is about!

Before registering for this intensive workshop, I made a commitment to myself to fully embrace every activity required, including moving meditation, yoga, and dancing. I handled most of it pretty well but became extremely self-conscious about dancing in public. How would I look when I literally let it all hang out?

Here's the deal: I am a *big* dancer, both physically and energetically. On the rare occasions when I dance in the way Spirit moves me—complete with arms flailing, big butt jiggling, and wide hips circling—nearby observers are advised to take cover as I may poke somebody's eye out. I'm not sure whether my predilection for wild tribal dancing is due to my Native American ancestry or to excessive teenage exposure to the 80s pop song "Relax" from Frankie Goes to Hollywood. Regardless of the reason, when the right music starts playing, my ass-wigglin' could give Charo or Shakira a run for their money.

However, since I've always been in the 'fat girl' category, I've never given myself full permission to totally let loose. For years dancing was embarrassing and uncomfortable, and I'd inevitably end up harshly judging my body and my sexuality. If I "had" to dance, I'd usually assess the social environment prior to stepping on the dance floor. How did my body compare to those around me? How freely do the other dancers move? Which outside observers would critique my performance? If I was out with friends at a packed club late at night with several tequila shots behind me, I could muster the courage to swivel my hips with utter abandon. On the other hand, if I was attending a wedding reception in a brightly lit banquet hall when the legendary "Brick House" started to play, I would dampen my dancing desire, assimilate with the rest of the pack, and execute the classic White Man Dance. Alas, another perfectly good groove wasted on my fragile self-esteem.

For years my passionate love for dancing remained largely suppressed because I feared the quiet (and most likely phantom) ridicule from strangers. After attending the recent workshop, however, my perception of my body changed forever. This transformational class helped participants honestly explore the serious issues most of us have—issues of safety, trust and acceptance. Each day included exercises in meditation, journaling, yoga, sharing our personal stories, and yes, dancing. We expressed deeply-hidden feelings through deliberate movement, exposing our fear, anger and joy with each tentative step. As I moved around the room I began to push through my lifelong inhibitions and seek out darker emotions that lay hidden underneath. Through this experience I learned a great deal about myself. I discovered how I let the opinions of strangers suppress my own joy, how drawing attention to my body made me feel unsafe, and how I was petrified of publicly displaying my sensuality.

As I continued to dance throughout the week, I stayed with these terrifying feelings. Eventually my fears turned into surrender that ultimately turned into bliss. Through my connection to Spirit, I arrived at a place where I could trust my body's wisdom and honor its desire for movement regardless of how it appeared to the outside world. Dancing in this conscious way allowed me to embrace my physical body and experience spiritual energy in a whole new way. I did what most of us dare not do: I unleashed my God-given mojo for all to see. And you know what? It felt pretty friggin' good! It was like getting stoned off my own power. Ironically, at the end of the workshop several participants told me how much they enjoyed watching me dance with such freedom and wished they could move like that. What a strange twist of fate it was to find myself being seen as a model for physical confidence instead of being the ignored wallflower I had allowed myself to be for so long.

Many of us have spent a lifetime sacrificing the pleasures of movement to the beast of judgment, and I, for one, am sick of it. From this moment on I am going to honor my big, beautiful, and powerful body whenever I have the opportunity to dance. I will shake and shimmy it wherever the music takes me, no matter where I am or whose eyes are on me! I *deserve* to experience the Divine ecstasy of dance and so, dear reader, do you.

THERAPY FOR MY COLON

⟡

I AM FULL OF SHIT. Literally. I discovered this truth when I had my colon professionally flushed at ten o'clock yesterday morning. Let me tell you, it sure was an eye-opener.

I have been on a diet for the last few months but haven't really lost the amount of weight expected given the paltry amount of food I had eaten and my high level of physical activity. I know our bodies change and metabolism slows as we age, but something was definitely amiss. It wasn't that I was freaking out about not losing more poundage; my bigger concern was the unshakable feeling that something wasn't right. My body felt like my fat was somehow holding on despite my valiant efforts at peacefully and lovingly removing it.

I had recently experienced several healing sessions pertaining to my body issues and felt confident that, for the most part, my sluggishness was not due to unprocessed emotions. My body just felt...stuck. This uneasy feeling started to manifest itself in, shall we say, excretion challenges. The more I meditated on what to do about my intestinal malaise, the clearer the guidance became: get colon therapy.

I sheepishly admit that it took about six weeks and many messages from Spirit, not to mention increasingly uncomfortable constipation, before I decided to bite the bullet and make the appointment. If you have ever subjected yourself to this nasty treatment I'm sure you can understand my procrastination. I don't know the exact physics of the procedure, nor do I want to, but I can confirm that warm water and plastic hoses stuck up my patootie were involved.

I recommend that you skip these next few paragraphs if you have a squeamish tummy. Trust me, honey, you'll thank me. At the beginning of the treatment the unpleasant physical sensations were minimal—basically mild discomfort akin to driving along the highway, having to use the bathroom, and being three exits away from the next rest stop. Annoying, to be sure, but not horrendous. As the session progressed, however, we reached more ancient, noxious deposits in the crevices of my colon. The sensations became more intense which caused me to stop my peaceful yogic breathing and start to moan in pain like my brother does after ingesting third helpings at Thanksgiving dinner. My cramps worsened, I broke out in cold sweats, and I came within a hair's breadth of horking all over the floor.

During the entire hour of my treatment I had an increasingly strong desire to poop, and apparently I did, in fact, poop for an hour. The therapist told me that I "released" (a more polite word for shat) upwards of eight to ten regular BMs. These weren't BMs from last night's salmon and broccoli dinner either; they were from old, nasty, toxic goo lodged in the pockets of my colon from God-only-knows how long ago. Ish!!!

Blessedly the nightmare eventually subsided, and I was *finally* allowed bathroom privileges. My experience in the loo that morning was akin to a Saturn V liftoff. After exiting ten minutes later, I felt as weak as a day-old kitten; however, within moments my strength returned. I began to not only feel good, but started to feel really, really good. I would go so far as to say I felt grrrrreat!

Based on my pre-treatment tutorial from Norma—you have to be on a first-name basis with someone who sticks a hose up your ass for an hour—as well as the information I learned during my days in massage school, I know that the colon is the waste receptacle of our bodies. If toxins hang around long enough, they can make us tired, bloated, overweight, and can be the welcoming committee for disease. My elimination stagnation was akin to adding bag upon bag to the garbage can without ever, *ever*, emptying it. Now there's a lovely image.

Traditional Chinese Medicine teaches us that our organs hold emotional stuff too. Since I had been focusing so much effort of late on processing my big, ugly, lifelong issues, I suspected this treatment would rock my world. I also guessed that there may have been sadness from my mother's recent passing lurking in an intestinal pocket or two. After the session, my suspicions were confirmed; I found myself consumed with profound grief for the rest of the day.

Even with the drama I endured yesterday, I was glad I got roto-rootered. I feel lighter both physically and energetically, and Norma thinks I could have easily pooped out five pounds. Yay! The procedure also made my body feel cleaner and more efficient. I'm planning on going back for another session next week and will most likely continue to do so until my vehicle starts working the way it was designed. To be sure, I'm not looking forward to the uncomfortable sensations (although Norma assures me it gets easier every time). I am, however, looking forward to taking better care of myself and "releasing" that which no longer serves me.

THE ANATOMY
OF A BINGE

LATELY I HAVE BEEN LIKE THE NEEDLE on a turntable, totally in the groove. It all started after getting colon therapy a few days ago. Ever since that intestinal blowout things had been going really well in every area of my life. I got on the scale and dropped another two pounds last week, totaling seventeen pounds in three months. Woo hoo! I received a killer massage and had an amazing acupuncture treatment, both of which I found to be very healing. My yoga and meditation practices had been wonderful. I helped a client whose son is stationed in Iraq begin to shift her focus from fear to trust. I counseled a dear friend and her family at the hospital, helping them to work through the initial shock of a cancer diagnosis. Last but not least, the magazine for which I wrote had just hit the stands, and it contained my best and most personal column yet. I felt healthy, connected, and powerful. Yeah, baby!

But then the other shoe fell. Suddenly, without warning, I took the express train to Funkville. I was about ready to hop into my car to pick up my daughter Emma from the bus stop when inexplicably my mood shifted from peaceful to panicked. I started to feel alone, depressed, and afraid. When faced with the onslaught of these emotions, I instinctively made a beeline for the kitchen.

Ninety-five percent of our pantry was stocked with healthy stuff completely unsuitable for bingeing, but there were a few naughty carbs designated for Emma's lunchbox that lurked on the bottom shelf. There they sat, quietly taunting me. On that particular day their call became deafening; the Cheez-its would not be ignored. I opened the box and quickly shoved several handfuls into my mouth. Yummmm.

The salty goodness of the Cheez-its started to make me feel a little better (or unconscious, to be more precise). Unfortunately, the savory orange squares hadn't entirely squelched my panic. I thought about what else I needed. Sweets! I needed something sugary. Remembering there was an open bag of Skittles hiding somewhere from a recent Rose Family Movie Night, I frantically searched for the red bag in the dark corners of the pantry. Searching...searching...yes! Found them! I poured all the remaining colorful balls of heaven into my hand and popped them into my salivating mouth. The binge had officially begun.

Running late due to my detour to Snacktown, I hurriedly got into my car and sped down the road obsessing over the prospect of sneaking in just one more treat before resuming my role as responsible Mommy. Let's see...I had crackers and candy. What else did I want? My mind raced as I thought of one last thing I could shovel into my mouth before Emma greeted me at the bus stop. Aha! Ice cream!

Buoyed by my stroke of bingeing ingenuity, I excitedly drove to the new ice cream shop that opened a few miles from our house. As I entered the hallowed halls of Haagen-Dazs, I became completely oblivious to anyone else in the shop. My eyes were fixed on the display case as I scanned the labels to identify the perfect antidote for my funk. Eureka! There it was, glistening in the glass. One of God's greatest combinations: chocolate and peanut butter. I giddily ordered a single scoop on a sugar cone and snarfed it down while sitting in my hot car in the parking lot. Afterwards I hastily removed all evidence of the crime except for the teeny Lady Macbeth-like brown splotch that stubbornly remained on my periwinkle shirt. (Karma sucks sometimes.)

I kicked into thespian mode upon seeing my little girl. On the outside, everything seemed perfectly normal. On the inside, however, a guilt-ridden tempest was brewing. As was typical with all post-binge periods, I secretly wallowed in shame for hours. When Michael came home from work I immediately confessed my sins, hoping my admission would free me from the remorse I felt.

Truth be told, the binge wasn't really that bad. I have experienced dozens of others lasting far longer and involving infinitely more calories. No, my guilt related to the lightning-fast pendulum swing from consciousness to numbness. Jeez, I thought I was doing so well! I had been working through my food and body acceptance issues with lots of healing work, yoga, reading, and writing. Writing. Writing? Hmmm. The light bulb started to flicker, and I began to grasp the "why" of the most recent binge.

My monthly column had just hit the streets. It was the one in which, for the first time, I openly shared my lifelong battle with food addiction. By then thousands of people would have read the ugly truth about My Biggest Issue. Many of the readers would appreciate my courage and relate to my story personally; in fact I had already started to receive praise for the piece. No matter. At that moment my fear was far bigger than my boldness. I feared there were people out there who would read it from a place of judgment and ridicule, having a good laugh at my expense. Had my biggest weakness become fodder for cruel jokes?

It was then that I fully realized the duality within me. When I revealed myself so completely and authentically through writing, I was at my joyful, creative peak. I was in alignment with my Divine purpose, my words inspired others to recognize their own power, and I experienced a catharsis more profound than any other therapy I have known. And...

When I revealed myself so completely and authentically through writing, I opened myself up to pain, judgment, and ridicule.

This awareness of my vulnerability was the true source of my afternoon binge. I had freaked out because my deep, dark secret was no longer a secret. It was *out there*, and there was no running away from it. This public "outing" made me feel fragile, alone, depressed, and afraid. To make matters worse, my feelings were magnified by the recent healing work I had received which had dramatically increased the energy running through me.

As I had done so many times before, I ran toward food like a Pavlovian dog to muffle the sounds of my own fear. The resultant food fog and corresponding downward spiral felt hauntingly familiar. Thankfully my ongoing spiritual work had taught me the only thing that truly silences the inner demon of fear is *trust*.

When I remembered to trust that Spirit unconditionally supports my writing, my healing process, and my life, I was able to let go of the need to control those things around me. I trusted that all would be well as long as I walked this world as truthfully and consciously as possible. I had been afraid of judgment and ridicule, yet I had so often judged and ridiculed others. By honestly looking at my behaviors, I had finally discovered the tough lessons of my binge. Stop judging myself. Stop judging others. Stop worrying about others judging me. Just live my truth and trust that it is all Divinely orchestrated.

When fear once again rears its ugly head, as I know it will, I know I no longer need to reach for food to protect myself. I can sink into the scary feelings, ground my energy into the earth, honestly look at my own choices, and humbly ask for help. I fundamentally trust that Spirit loves, guides and protects me in every single moment as It does for you and every other person on this planet. There is great comfort in having that kind of support that carbs and candy simply can't provide.

I am looking forward to a life where I can occasionally enjoy Skittles, Cheez-its and Haagen-Dazs without spiraling into a binge or landing in an emotional funk. They are, after all, tasty and satisfying treats, especially when they aren't partnered with heaping servings of fear, guilt and shame.

It's Only a Number

PLATEAU. This simple word strikes fear in the hearts and hips of dieters everywhere. If you are one of those blessed souls that have never dieted, you may never have heard the word 'plateau' used in a diet context. The rest of us "losers" know that hitting a plateau means that no matter what actions are taken, the pounds simply aren't coming off. After four months of near devotional commitment to my weight loss regimen, I have found myself smack-dab in the middle of the Mother of All Plateaus.

Earlier this year, as I weighed-in at 175 pounds, I finally decided to commence the last and greatest battle with the bulge. Even writing that number sends ripples of shame throughout my body. I suppose I could look at the bright side. Six years ago I tipped the scales at over a deuce at my post-baby, all-time heaviest and roundest. No matter how radiant the glow of new motherhood, hefting around 200+ pounds on my statuesque 5'3" frame was *not* a pretty sight.

When I started down my healing path earlier this year, I vowed I would do anything, *anything*, to release my lifelong albatross of fat. The reward for all the work I had done was the loss of twenty pounds. (Yay Me!) Yet, over the last six weeks the number on the bathroom scale has not budged: 153. This number has been par-

ticularly difficult to see every day as it was the same number chart-
ed in the little box labeled "Starting Weight" in my first Weight
Watchers diet log twenty-five years ago. The weight of 153 is forever emblazoned in my psyche as a symbol of failure, weakness,
addiction, and ugliness. A quarter of a century later, I still can't
escape that friggin' number.

I have come a long way towards accepting my body as a reflection of the Divine since those early days of dieting and deprivation.
I know I don't need to be pencil-thin to be beautiful or worthwhile.
Through my wiser and more compassionate eyes, I would be more
than willing to accept 153 as my ideal weight but for one teeny,
tiny thing—I don't *feel* well. I am constantly bloated and feel like
I am sporting a Michelin tire around my midsection. My digestive
and elimination systems are completely out of whack despite the
copious amounts of fruit, fish oils, and fiber I ingest on a daily
basis. There is a *huge* gulf between what I am taking into my body
and what is coming out. To put it bluntly, I feel like crap because I
rarely take one.

My perpetual state of 'too-fullness' has affected my mood, my
sleep, and the most precious of treasures, my sex life. After enduring several days without so much as a rabbit turd exiting my
overstuffed bod, I have recently chosen to give myself enemas as
a last-ditch effort to get things moving. Since I have no desire for
a permanent relationship with these plastic gizmos, I am getting a
wee bit antsy for a peaceful and rapid conclusion to my intestinal
drama.

As a professional dieter, I know all too well the specific techniques one employs to break through a weight loss plateau. I can
regurgitate in excruciating detail the advice I have repeatedly, and
sometimes condescendingly, received from a multitude of perky
Jenny Watchers weight-loss professionals from times past. "Change
the times you eat! Don't eat after 6pm! Eat different foods! Eat
smaller meals throughout the day! Exercise more often! Cut out
any empty-calorie snacks! Drink more water! Change up your

workout routine!" After exhausting all of these strategies, I realized that my issues are deeper and nastier than any weak-ass, Snackwells cookie-cutter approach to plateau-busting.

Earlier this week I was nearly in tears when I saw Shaun, my Acupuncture Physician, for my weekly needling. After spewing my emotional ick all over her beautifully appointed, Zen-like reception area, I begged her to enlighten me as to what I was doing "wrong". In her attempt to solve my riddle she asked me to describe everything I had been doing to lose weight. Well, let's see. Where do I start? How 'bout if I just make you a list? Beyond my weekly acupuncture sessions specifically addressing weight loss, I have been:

- Consuming small portions of mostly organic fruits and vegetables with very little starch, no red meat, no processed foods, no caffeine, and no refined sugar
- Drinking up to 100 ounces of water daily
- Swallowing all manner of metabolism-boosting and parasite killing Chinese herbs several times a day
- Soaking my tootsies in a detoxifying ionic foot bath once a week
- Practicing yoga five times a week
- Doing aerobic exercise with post-workout steams at least four times a week
- Receiving crystal bowl sound healings from my dearest hubby
- Enduring incredibly uncomfortable colonics every week at the capable hands of Norma, the sweetest inflicter of torture I've ever known
- Getting regular bodywork treatments of massage therapy and energy work

All these efforts are over and above the daily meditations, affirmations and visualizations designed to bring my body back into harmony. In these sessions I frequently have in-depth discussions with my cells, organs and systems where I honor the important roles they play, express gratitude for their efforts, and generally love 'em up more than I did my first kitten. Despite my quasi-obsessive healing efforts, the scale remained fixed on 153 and my colon remained stuck.

Blessedly, things began to shift after receiving a massage a few days later. My massage therapist is Robert, an incredibly powerful, gifted and intuitive healer trapped in the body of a Greek god. (I try not to think about his off-the-charts cuteness factor when I'm naked under the sheet; it's far too distracting.) After our last session, Young Master Robert shared the guidance he received when attempting to massage the Michelin tire located in my abdomen.

Rob told me he thought my body had gone into lock-down mode in response to a seemingly endless wave of loss. He reminded me of the major changes that have occurred over the last nine months: my mother died, my grandfather died, I closed my business which, in turn, ended several dear friendships and a long-standing dream, I stopped my energy healing private practice, I quit my various teaching gigs, and my best friend moved across the country. Whether I initiated these life events or they were simply the result of the inevitable circle of life, it was clearly a lot of change for me to process (or not to process as the case may be). I was handling each transition as quickly and healthfully as possible, but my body was simply not *ready* to let go of the weight too.

Rob's words rang true for me, and I began to sympathize with my belly instead of angrily cursing it. While not yet changing the scale or my bathroom woes, the insight he provided gave me some much-needed clarity and comfort. My physical body was trying to serve as my protector while feverishly trying to play catch-up to the progress I had made mentally, emotionally and spiritually. It was high time I quit chastising myself for failing to perform. Rather, I needed to gently and lovingly acknowledge how truly difficult the last year had been.

Even with my new awareness I am still holding steady at 153 pounds. Sure, 153 isn't the number I'm thrilled to see, but it's the one that is here today. Most likely it will be that same number tomorrow. But someday, when my body catches up to my mind and spirit, the number will eventually go down. (I hope!) Until then, I'll keep lovin' up my Michelin middle and stop fretting about what digits show up on my bathroom scale. I am finally starting to accept that I am now, I have always been, and I will always be, so much more than a number.

THE FACE OF THE DEVIL

&

I BELIEVE IN THE DEVIL. Mine is not the traditional red-suit wearing, pitchfork-toting figure of childhood lore, but rather a more conventional creature that lurks in the most benign of places. My version of Lucifer sits on the tile floor, has an LCD display, and takes root in our fears and shame. In my world, the devil and his pitchfork come in the form of the bathroom scale.

Throughout my history of emotional overeating and deprivation dieting, I have often succumbed to the power of this mighty demon. The number it displayed on any given day told me what to think of myself and dictated my mood du jour. Recognizing the vise grip this seemingly innocuous device has had on me is one of the critical keys to my healing process.

After residing in the previously mentioned Mother of All Plateaus for what seemed like years, I decided to take a revolutionary approach to bust through it. Instead of attacking my stalled progress with more intensity, dedication, and physical effort, I took the opposite tact. If I was getting sick and tired of seeing 153 on that horrendous machine every day, then there was a simple solution to my problem. I mustered enough strength to intentionally break the Dieter's First Commandment: Thou Shalt Weigh Thyself Regularly to Measure Thy Progress.

Refusing to weigh myself was difficult for me at first. I was desperately seeking the much-deserved kudos for the great choices I had been making. It was easy to ignore the devil when I was binge eating, avoiding mirrors, and wearing tent-like fashions; it was a lot more difficult to ignore it when I was eating healthy, exercising, and focusing on releasing my inner emotional garbage. I have needed an iron will to refuse its validating display, but I am happy to report that as of this writing I have no earthly idea how much I weigh.

My boycott of the scale has already elicited some very welcome results. First and foremost, I am confident I have pushed through that God-forsaken plateau, since all of my clothes are now much looser on me. In fact, my now-baggy wardrobe prompted me to go on another shopping excursion. (This one was a *lot* more pleasant than the Target judge fest I went on several months ago.) What a joyous experience is was to buy cute clothes in a size other than an XL or above! Yay! Life is good. Even better than shopping for clothes that actually fit me are the romantic perks. During one of our recent carnal forays, Michael lovingly told me that there was now less of me to love so he'd need to love the rest of me even more. Ahhh...the man's words were dulcet tones to my soul.

The utter disregard I have shown the measurement beast is a major contributor to my shrinking size and newfound body acceptance. However, my digital 'dis' has also brought with it a cruel irony: I have no idea how much weight I've lost. As someone who has spent her entire life letting a number on the scale determine her self-worth, not knowing the 'pounds lost' and 'pounds to go' numbers is unnerving to say the very least. Historically, I would always know how close I was to the coveted "goal weight". Did I have 20, 30, 40, 50 or more pounds to lose? Now that I am finally *in* my body and experiencing the utopic lifestyle change to which all dieters fantasize, I have no freakin' clue how close I am to reaching Goal Weight Nirvana.

When I am at the gym, the elliptical cardio equipment constantly reminds me of my ignorance. Upon stepping on its pedals, the machine asks me how much I weigh. Each time I see the question, a strange mix of annoyance, curiosity, and dread washes over me. What *is* my weight anyway? I sheepishly keep entering 150 because a part of me is afraid to guess at a lighter weight, even to my impartial friend. I have an irrational fear that the little red dots on its display will come back and say, "Try again, honey. You are *so* not 140 pounds."

After my workouts, I enter the locker room and see the Detecto industrial-size scale staring back at me. Each and every day Detecto calls to me, and each and every time I pass it by. A major reason why I ignore Detecto is the negative effect it clearly has on my body-conscious sisters who make the same mistake I used to. They step on that wretched machine, anxiously await the verdict, and allow the numeric result to control how they feel about themselves. I have observed wave after wave of self-hate flood these gorgeous women because the numbers aren't what they were hoping for. Their confidence, their life force, and their joy are sapped by the number the steely devil reveals. Frankly, this pisses me off. That silly piece of metal should not wield so much power over so many Divine creatures.

In that spirit, I declare that I no longer want to lose weight! That very statement of 'losing weight' makes my fat sound like a misplaced gem that will eventually be found in the future. I've lost and found lots of weight far too many times; I am now ready to release it forever, not just temporarily misplace it. This change in mindset has brought me to love all aspects of my body, and the bitter relationship with the scale is simply unnecessary.

My bathroom scale is now safely tucked away where it can no longer harm anyone. Naturally there is a part of me that would *love* to see the small numbers shining back at me—numbers I have dreamed of seeing my whole life—but the validation just isn't worth the price I would have to pay. I like how it feels to be free from the beast's crushing grip. My body feels absolutely wonderful and I am finally starting to accept myself fully and completely. This is indeed cause for celebration!

However, the devil doesn't like joyous celebrations. It wants me to feel nervous and fearful about my weight. It wants me to feel ashamed of my body. It wants me to compare my numbers to those of my sisters. I am at war with this devil of fear, doubt, and shame. I've lost a lot of fights over the years, but I am determined to be the ultimate victor. My inner battles are fought one day at a time, one choice at a time.

I predict another large-scale conflict will occur several months from now. I will have to step on a Detecto for my annual physical exam. My strategy is to confidently step on the scale, ask the nurse's assistant to keep the results to herself, and maybe, just maybe, get through the whole process without sneaking a quick one-eyed peek at the number. Maybe.

War is hell.

COMING OUT OF THE SMOKE-FILLED CLOSET

CAPRI ULTRA LIGHT MENTHOLS. My cigarettes of choice were as thin as pencils and had a minty aftertaste. I rationalized that smoking these petite chick-cigs was almost like not smoking at all! At the very least they were far less odious than the Marlboro Lights I first smoked as a teenager. I secretly smoked off and on—mostly on—for over twenty years, shamefully hiding my habit from my husband, child, family, friends, and clients. How's that for enlightened?

I had my first cigarette in seventh grade. At thirteen years of age, I was immersed in a world of teenage misery that included raging hormones, social angst, and a new stepfather. My escape was found in the welcoming arms of the older crowd known as the "burnouts". One day after school, a fellow stoner offered me one of his Marlboro Lights from the crumpled white box he kept in his back pocket. That first Marlboro Light tasted horrible, yet its emotional lure was undeniable. When I held it between my index and middle finger, I felt cool, accepted, a part of the club, all grown up. Unfortunately, just like millions of other children who pick up their first cigarette, I picked up another. And another. Soon after the taste of the cigarettes changed from horrible to good. Nurse, note the time: a new addiction is born.

In my teens and early twenties, I often went from smoker to non-smoker with relative ease. If I wasn't socializing with smokers, I wouldn't smoke. If I was, I would. My mother was also a smoker, but I secretly hid my habit from her for years. She would often beg me to never start lighting up. Embarrassed by my weakness, I lied to her face and assured her I would never do such a thing. Hours later I'd be out with my friends puffing away.

I have lied and covered up my addiction countless times to countless people. When Michael and I were dating he once told me he wouldn't be in a relationship with a woman who smoked. I believe "showstopper" was the word he used. Petrified of losing the best thing that ever happened to me, I immediately decided to quit (or suspend) my smoking habit. I kept my dirty secret from the man I love because I feared the worst; that he would end our relationship if he knew about my habit.

Somewhere along the line I lit up once again, but even more surreptitiously now that I had a husband to navigate around. I can't even remember when I had that first cigarette after going without one for so long. Most likely it was during one of the many grueling business trips I took as a technology consultant. Over the next several years my habit would repeatedly wax and wane depending on my anxiety and depression levels at the time.

At one point Mom found out I smoked. She was so disappointed that I had taken on the same monkey she had. She told me it broke her heart to see me with a cigarette in my hand. Nevertheless, the two of us started smoking around each other whenever the opportunity presented itself. In fact, in a twisted sort of way it was one of the ways we bonded. Our shared nicotine addictions were a rare commonality, and I truly enjoyed our peaceful, if stinky, smoke-fests together. All of this covert activity was still unbeknownst to my husband and daughter.

Any addict can confirm that the experience of smoking (or any other compulsion) is so much more than the physical act itself. These tiny tobacco sticks took on a life of their own, and I established a long-running relationship with them. As with any close relationship, daily rituals emerged with Capri and me. My little sticks accompanied me while driving, capped-off a delicious meal (when I was able to sneak away), helped me to relax, and made the occasional cocktail taste a little better. The addiction, like a manipulative lover, convinced me that I was powerless without it.

About a week before Mom got diagnosed with lung cancer, she and I had a conversation about smoking. After admitting she wasn't feeling well, she remarked, "I really need to quit this time." My mom had tried to quit many times before, and each failed attempt brought with it more self-judgment and bitter resentment. Since I was in the alternative healing profession she asked me for advice on the best way to quit. (I found it strange that she asked advice from the woman who was a walking poster child for addiction.) I told her she needed to look at the deeper root causes of her smoking instead of just addressing the physical cessation with a patch or a pill. In the same conversation she confided in me that cigarettes were "always there for her" and "the only things that never let her down". How on earth could my mother quit something that never let her down? Why would she *want* to? Sadly, she never did.

After Mom got diagnosed, I immediately stopped smoking (yet again) and promised her I would never pick up another cigarette. I kept my promise for months until the stress of her illness and impending death became so overwhelming that I decided to have "just one" to calm my frayed nerves. BAD IDEA. I should have known better; it is *never* just one. Riddled with shame, I hid my habit from her by secretly smoking in the back of her house while she lay in bed. I painfully recall the moments where I wanted to have my Capri more than spend time with my dying mother. Those lost minutes I can never get back. That's how cruel and powerful addictions can become.

As I continued to chain-smoke during the last month of her ill-ness, I convinced myself I couldn't give it up until after she died. I moved the 'quit date' three more times before I actually did it for good. I'd solemnly vow, "I'll quit after the memorials", "I'll quit after I've finished cleaning out her house", and "I'll quit after the first of the year." Each time I'd feel increasingly guilty for making another empty "I'll quit after..." promise.

In January of 2007, six weeks after Mom died, I took a few days off with my friend, Jean. She and I worked our butts off during the previous month closing down Mom's house and needed some time to recover, both physically and emotionally. My latest empty prom-ise was to quit smoking after I returned from the trip. But some-thing unexpected happened that made me a non-smoker forever.

We were staying at a fabulous holistic spa in Miami. The high-light of the facility is a sacred room called the Hamam, a Turkish communal bath and steam area. The energy of this room is incredi-ble! Each day I spent many hours in the Hamam feeling very peace-ful and connected to Spirit. After speaking with several members of the staff, I learned that the owner is a very spiritual person who intended the Hamam to be a powerful energy vortex. The room was designed by premier Feng Shui consultants and blessed by a group of Tibetan monks.

Throughout the trip I spent several hours meditating in the Hamam, asking Spirit to help me process my grief and get my life back on track. During one particularly intense meditation session, I went inside my body with my mind's eye and traveled through each of my organs to see if there was any illness or disease that needed healing. When I got to my lungs I felt the same familiar sensations I had encountered when I worked on my mother: can-cer. I didn't know if I actually had cancer already or if it was in the process of being created. Regardless, I knew I had to choose *that moment* to do something about the disease or it would eventually take my life as well.

In my deep meditative state I humbly asked Spirit to heal me of the cancer that was starting to take hold in my body. In an instant I felt a wave of light pour through me from head to toe, as if my insides were being power-washed by loving, healing energy. This experience seemed to last no more than five minutes, but it felt like a blissful eternity. When it was complete I was so grateful for having received the amazing healing. After thanking Spirit, I asked what I could do as an offering of gratitude. The message came back clearly and without hesitation: quit smoking right now. Make the last cigarette you had be the last one you'll ever have. Don't quit tomorrow or next week. Quit *now*.

Spirit told me if I wanted to remain healthy I needed to appropriately honor the experience I just had. I could continue to smoke if I wanted to, but the healing I had just received would not be permanent. Spirit's message was not at all threatening; rather, it was very clear and matter-of-fact. If I wanted to accept the healing, I would quit smoking. Or not. It was entirely my choice.

As I sat on the heated marble steps of the Hamam, my cigarette addiction swiftly departed. I no longer felt I *had* to quit smoking for my health, my family, clients, or social acceptance. Instead, I truly *wanted* to quit smoking to show my respect and gratitude to Spirit. Simply changing my viewpoint from having to quit to wanting to quit changed the way I looked at smoking forever. I simply don't want to do it anymore.

Since that day I have been in hundreds of situations that used to trigger my desire to light up and had many opportunities to do so. Each time I am in one of those situations, I think about that magical day when Spirit wiped the slate clean for me. I made a promise and have absolutely no desire to go back on my word.

I am totally convinced I received a profound healing from Spirit that day. But even if it was all a steam-induced hallucination, the results are still the same. Because of what happened to me in that Miami steam room, I chose to no longer be a victim to cigarettes. I chose to reclaim my power from addiction. I chose to have a longer, healthier life. I am so grateful I am no longer a closet smoker hiding in the shadows wracked with guilt! In my heart, I know my mother witnessed the entire blessed event from above and beamed with pride when her little girl finally, *finally*, chucked the monkey.

LOVE & SEX

"Anyone can be passionate,
but it takes real lovers to be silly."

—ROSE FRANKEN

THE UNSEXY SIDE OF SEX

☙

I'LL BE HONEST—I'm a great lay. I can state with reasonable certainty based on a wealth of data gathered over the last twenty-five years that I am, in fact, fabulous in the sack. Before you dismiss my claim as the delusional ramblings of an almost-middle-aged woman with an oversized ego, hear me out. My facility for fornication was not born out of want but out of need, and it was carefully cultivated for the emotional benefits I received. I learned early on in life, far too early, that being good in bed meant receiving attention and affection that otherwise would have passed me by.

I have been at odds with my sexuality since puberty. At twelve I was an early, if not the first, bloomer in my class. The nearly instantaneous arrival of my attention-grabbing breasts was met with fierce derision from the other girls and paralyzing fear from the boys. I responded by wearing an absurd amount of clothing, hoping the sheer volume of material would camouflage my mounds. Nearly every day, regardless of the weather, I would wear a bra, t-shirt, Oxford button-down shirt and thick knit sweater to hide my femaleness. Jack, the fiendish class clown, sat in the desk behind me. Channelling Satan himself, he maneuvered through all the layers and viciously snapped my bra—*every friggin' day*. But, hey, I'm not bitter.

Somewhere between the ages of twelve and fifteen, the sexual dynamics between boys and girls started to change. Girls began showing interest in boys, and the boys started choosing which girls were worthy of them. While I was a member of the semi-popular clique, I was also cursed with the three Bs—brunette, brainy and bulky. It seemed I was forever destined to observe the dating game from the sidelines as the thinner, prettier girls were selected to play. If I was going to get any male attention whatsoever, it was clear I needed to take drastic measures. Like a human onion, I began to shed my layers, allowing my sequestered breasts to emerge and take center stage.

For the next ten years I accentuated my positives with tight t-shirts and revealing necklines, doing my best to stay in the game of competitive man-catching. (Personally, I think this should be added to the roster of Olympic sporting events.) I viewed intimacy and "making love" as the romantic fantasies of gullible ninnies, and I wasn't about to fall victim. Deciding to take a more callous, primal, and hedonistic approach to sex, I utilized it as one would prescription medicine. If my personal life was in crisis, my loneliness and depression unmanageable, or my self-esteem at a critical low, I would numb the pain with some chandelier-swinging romps.

During those years as a struggling single, I also discovered that possessing a bawdy sense of humor, consuming massive amounts of alcohol, and grinding to the popular techno-song du jour would deliver some male companionship rather quickly. After downing a drink called a Blowjob (a wretched concoction of Kahlua, Bailey's and whipped cream chugged from a shot glass) with my hands tied behind my back, I would invariably attract a horn-dog or two ready to learn what other interesting talents I had. I'm sure my mother would have been proud to know that I've received more than one drunken marriage proposal after performing this cute little parlor trick.

The act of sex made me feel pretty, important, and desired, even if it was for only the night (or the hour). I soon discovered that my contentment was directly proportional to my skill as a sexpot.

In my desperate and futile attempts to morph a booty call into a real relationship, I continually expanded my carnal repertoire and regularly performed an O-Dance similar to Meg Ryan's infamous faux orgasm in *When Harry Met Sally*.

This was me at my un-sexiest. Instead of meeting Mr. Right, I often toyed with Mr. Right Now. None of these guys were the great loves of my life—several were emotionally unhealthy, chemically addicted, financially challenged, mentally dim, and/or already in "committed" relationships. Ultimately it didn't really matter who was next to me in bed as long as his fleeting touch helped quiet the self-hating critic inside my head.

There were, however, a few brief and beautiful flashes of love. I fondly recall two of my earliest relationships, both of which were with caring, sweet and wonderful young guys who loved the dickens out of me. Alas, fate brought one relationship to a close and a poor selfish choice ended the other.

Aside from these notable exceptions, the majority of my partnerships were little more than meaningless after-party hook-ups. This pattern continued unabated until 1995. I was at my all-time low having recently relocated to Denver. My mother, the guy I adored, and all of my closest friends were a thousand miles away in Chicago. On the work front, I was feverishly climbing the corporate ladder, working a ridiculous amount of hours, and facing routine sexual harassment at the hands of my boss. On top of it all, I was embroiled in yet another complicated and hurtful "friendship with benefits" with a co-worker. Each day was filled with growing depression and loneliness.

Mercifully, an angel came into my life. Her name was Jan, and she was a gifted psychotherapist. I started seeing Jan every Tuesday night to deal with my sexual harassment. However, not long after the sessions began, lots of other nasty stuff came up, things I had previously held under lock and key. Jan helped me give voice to many painful truths about the alcoholism in my family, my parents' divorce, multiple incidents of molestation, and several other sensitive issues. We also talked openly about my sexuality and Jan taught me how my sexual promiscuity was about more than getting attention; it was a natural response to untreated trauma. It was in those Tuesday night crying, screaming, swearing sessions that started my healing journey that continues to this day.

It horrifies me when I reflect on my slew of unsavory sexual experiences prior to meeting Michael. Somehow through the grace of God, I escaped that period without getting sick, pregnant, or killed. But I paid a price nonetheless. I am acutely aware of how little I valued myself as a human being. It would have been nice to have had the strength to say "No, thank you" to the paltry offerings at the boyfriend buffet and wait for the right one rather than giving myself away so cheaply. There's a part of me that would love to be able to erase my seedy history from memory, not only my own but those of my many partners. Unfortunately, the brain isn't like a hard drive that can be reformatted to start from scratch.

Truth be told, if I were somehow given the chance to expunge these exploits from my history book I probably wouldn't want to anyway. Despite my colorful and embarrassing past I am grateful for every single sordid affair. Having what I *didn't* want ultimately enabled me to see clearly what I *did* want. As with everything, those experiences contributed in some way to the woman I am now and the amazing life I enjoy.

Fairy tales always have heroes and villains, and in my fairy tale, I served as my own sexual villain for many years. Thankfully, Spirit interceded and helped me to conquer this foe through the slow, arduous process of emotional repair. Eventually I started to value myself a little more and through that growth, I found the prince of my dreams. Bucking conventional wisdom, our marriage and love-making are better now than they were a decade ago when I walked down the aisle. Through honesty, openness, and trust, my prince and I have created a sex life that is real, powerful, and crazy/good. After kissing a whole lot of frogs, I am finally living, and loving, happily ever after. Now *that's* sexy.

I Chased Him
'Til He Caught Me

CB

"**F**EEL THE FEAR AND DO IT ANYWAY" was one of my mother's favorite inspirational quotes. She had an unlimited supply of one-liners she'd whip out on any occasion requiring steely reserve or a boost of confidence. "This too shall pass" and "What doesn't kill you makes you stronger" were also liberally dispensed in my childhood home. A little over a decade ago I found myself feeling the fear and doing it anyway when I jumped headfirst into the deep end of the relationship pool.

In the fall of 1995, I was working for a major corporation in Denver managing software development projects. On a Monday afternoon in September of that year, Michael A. Rose rocked my world for the first time. I met my future husband in one of the many mind-numbing project meetings we were forced to attend. He sat at the opposite end of the conference table looking a helluva lot smarter and sexier than any of the other computer geeks I had seen there before.

I kept wondering, "Who is this cutie with the silver hair and devilish smile?" I eventually discovered that he was assigned to one of my projects. Hallelujah! That's Michael Rose from the East Coast consulting firm we had recently contracted! Yum yum. It looked like the latest project I was dreading just got a lot more interesting.

For the next several months, Michael and I worked closely together, including many late nights and weekends. Our working relationship grew into a friendship that eventually became a tentative romance. (Yep, I committed the big no-no of mixing business with pleasure.) Our first date was the company holiday party; I invited him. Subsequently we went on a few more dates including an idyllic picnic in the mountains.

The more time I spent with Michael, the goofier I behaved. I just wasn't the same person around him that I had been with other men. Normally I wore a fierce suit of armor, held my feelings firmly in check, and had a rather cynical outlook on love. When it came to relationships, my mantra was always, "Do it to them before they do it to you." Yet, whenever Michael was around I became a total girlie-girl. One of my cubicle buddies once commented that she always knew when I was on the phone with him because my voice went up an octave and I giggled throughout the call. Trust me on this: I was *not* a giggler by nature.

To put it bluntly, I fell hard and fast. Michael was smart, funny, interesting, sensitive, and absolutely adorable. There was just one little drawback—he lived across the country in Washington, DC. When the project ended, so would our relationship. I tried to convince myself to simply enjoy the remaining time he and I had together. However, I found myself frustrated with my growing affection for this amazing guy who I would have to say goodbye to in a matter of weeks. There wasn't much I could do to change the two-ships-passing-in-the-night scenario, although I did generate hundreds of useless new project "requirements" to keep him in town a few months longer than his original contract specified. Management had its privileges.

During the final weeks of the project, Michael and I were becoming ever closer. We loved hanging out together and would spend hours talking about our beliefs, dreams, family dramas, and past romantic dalliances. Things were going so well that we began to toy around with the idea of seeing each other after the project was over. We entertained the possibility of having a long-distance relationship, but neither one of us really had the stomach for it; they suck even in the best of circumstances. Moreover, we were both focusing on healing some old wounds and had no intention of getting back into another hot and heavy romance at the time. Logic dictated we go our separate ways, but there was something about the two of us that could not be ignored. Me and Mr. Rose had a thing goin' on.

Two weeks before the end of the project, we made a knee-jerk decision to spend one last weekend together in Washington, DC doing the tourist thing and preparing for our tearful *au revoir.* Days before embarking on the trip out east, I was a nervous wreck. I had fallen in love with Michael and was wracking my brain to figure out some way to keep him in my life. We were just getting to know each other outside of work, and I was heartsick at the thought of having the man of my dreams slip through my fingers. A day before getting on the airplane, I had an epiphany: If I love him that much (or think I will grow to), then I had to have the balls to do whatever it took to hold on to him. I knew what that meant: I would have to move to Washington, DC. Yikes!

In that moment, fear overtook me. What if he rejects me? What if he doesn't feel the same way? What if he turns out to be a jerk? What will everyone say? What if I can't find a job? What if I move there and he breaks up with me, leaving me in a strange town where I don't know a soul? The more I thought about moving to the East Coast, the scarier the voices inside my head became.

Despite my anxiety and panic, I somehow found a way to pack an overnight bag and catch the flight to Dulles Airport. The first day of our trip was a total blur since I was preoccupied with my ongoing mental duel. One minute I'd tell myself, "Forget it! Just let it go! You'll find someone else! Don't be a fool!" and the next minute I'd say, "Come on! This is your soulmate, dammit! Don't blow it! It's your once-in-a-lifetime chance!" My fear of rejection was doing battle with my desire for love, and I had no idea which side was going to prevail.

That Saturday night, Michael took me to an exotic Ethiopian restaurant in the Adams Morgan neighborhood of DC. While enjoying our delicious spicy stew I decided it was going to be now or never—I needed to find my cajones. I took a deep breath, drank a swig of beer, and dropped the bomb: "Why don't I move back here with you so we can make a go of this thing?" My question was met with stunned silence.

Michael was so shocked at my proposal that it rendered him nearly speechless for hours. As you can imagine, his silence did wonders for my eggshell-fragile self-esteem. The next day he recovered his verbal faculties enough to cautiously agree to my offer, much to my relief. I was, however, mildly PO'd at him for not immediately jumping up and down in the restaurant shouting, "Yes, yes, a thousand times yes!" to the delight of our fellow dining patrons. After all, that was how it was written in *my* version of the script.

Over that one weekend, our carefree fling had officially graduated to a serious, grown-up relationship. Without much thought or discussion, we agreed to take the big plunge and move in together. When we returned to Colorado, my family, friends and co-workers were all shocked at our sudden announcement. My mother was so blown away at my bold and uncharacteristic decision that she forgot to get angry about it. Yet no one was more freaked out than me by my spontaneous and downright ballsy decision to move across the country to a new city with no job, no friends, and a new, relatively unknown boyfriend.

This wasn't like me! I didn't just pick up and move for some guy I barely even knew. I was a Type-A planner, organizer, and list-maker who needed to have all of my ducks in a row before I would commence a project of that magnitude. I certainly wasn't the type to openly risk rejection at the hands of some man. But none of those things mattered when it came to Michael. He was worth the huge risks I was about to take. This gorgeous stud with the silver hair and the warm heart was simply too good to let slip away. Because of him I was living a happier life; I *had* to take a big risk for this one.

A few days later Michael and I packed up all of my stuff that hadn't either been sold or given away and loaded it into my beat-up Oldsmobile for our terrifying, yet exhilarating, cross-country road trip. Once we settled into his house and were no longer living our corporate roles, he and I quickly discovered how incredible it was to be madly in love with one's best friend. Four months later Michael proposed to me in a horse-drawn carriage in New York's Central Park (I said 'Yes' right away instead of making him wait a full day like he did). Ten months later, we got hitched.

One of the greatest lessons I learned from my drama in DC is the power of doing things that scare the daylights out of me. Playing it safe typically brings with it only boredom and mediocrity. On the other hand, having the courage to travel into previously uncharted territory can create remarkable opportunities full of joy, passion, and adventure.

I'm the first to admit that I am no expert in matters of the heart, nor do I possess the magic recipe for The Perfect Marriage. But what I do know is this: I found and married a fabulous man whom I adore, and I know that my ballsiness was a major contributing factor. Our beautiful partnership came about because I did those things I hadn't done before—I followed the energetic signs, trusted in Spirit to guide my way, moved through my fear, and most importantly, *risked*. As we have so often heard, big risks often generate big rewards.

If you are in a wonderful, fulfilling romance, congratulations! You rock. If so, why don't you take a moment to express some gratitude to your lover and your Higher Power for the gift of love you have received? If true love isn't a part of your life right now, I invite you to ask yourself one question: is there something or someone calling out for you to stop playing it safe and start taking some risks? You can take it from me; romantic bliss may be just around the corner if you have the guts to make the first move.

THE CURSE OF HAVING
A HOTTIE FOR A HUSBAND

M
Y HUSBAND LOOKS LIKE RICHARD GERE. Seriously. Strangers often comment on the uncanny resemblance Michael shares with the melt-in-your-mouth superhottie from *Pretty Woman*. Among Michael's many outstanding attributes are his intensely penetrating eyes, a warm smile, and insanely beautiful salt and pepper hair that makes women swoon. As a successful financial advisor Michael wears designer suits, tailored shirts, and stylish silk ties. He looks like he belongs on the cover of *GQ* instead of in an office. Oh yeah, I almost forgot to mention that he's powerful, funny, sensitive, caring, smart, and spiritual. But other than that, he's nothing to write home about.

Being married to this specimen of male greatness is a supreme blessing to me, but for years it was also a curse. During the first few years of our marriage I couldn't contain my jealousy. The ugly, green-eyed monster was a frequent presence in our home and the biggest challenge we faced.

On good days I would merely be curious about his client meetings, innocently inquiring about the women with whom he met or spoke to on the phone. On bad days I'd conduct my own little

Inquisition, digging for the smallest details about his innocuous interactions with the opposite sex. A typical interrogation would sound something like this: "What does she look like?", "Is she thin?", "Is she married?", "Do you think she's pretty?", and "Did she flirt with you?" Frankly, I don't know how he put up with my bullshit for as long as he did.

The most annoying thing about my jealousy was that it was completely baseless. Most of the time Michael couldn't even describe these phantom threats in pumps which, of course, aggravated me to no end. Even when he did, it still didn't matter as he is fundamentally a man of integrity and fidelity. These facts didn't stop me from seeing my replacement around every corner.

Things got even worse when he went to work for a large regional bank where the female to male ratio was basically a kajillion to one. Of the plethora of women that surrounded my spouse each day, at least half of them were smitten with him on some level. Don't ask me how I knew this; I just did. I was very familiar with how charming he could be and how females young and old would get school-girl giddy around him. I should know—I did the same damn thing when I met the guy. Michael, as usual, was completely clueless about the crushes he provoked. But his lack of awareness had absolutely no effect on my ever-present fear.

I believe my husband's appeal is compounded by the sad fact that so many women have partners who are emotionally AWOL. While these men love their wives and provide for their families, they rarely take the time or have the initiative to make their partners feel special. After years of marriage many of them don't really listen to their wives and show little interest in their thoughts, feelings and daily activities. ESPN often gets more attention than their spouses do. In contrast, Michael not only listens to and appreciates me, but also naturally does so for others. This makes him attractive indeed.

Like a hurricane traveling over land, my jealous streak eventually weakened over time. The fear of losing him to someone prettier, smarter, and just plain better dissipated for several reasons. First, I had sessions with highly-skilled practitioners of massage therapy, spiritual counseling, shamanic healing and energy work to address my negative self-image. Second, I began to energize my connection with the Divine and learned how to trust in Spirit, Michael, and most importantly, myself. Third, we leaned on each other in the midst of many hardships and challenges. With unwavering mutual support we faced the passing of family members, multiple career changes, several moves, my pregnancy and the birth of our daughter. Our partnership solidified and deepened through these shared experiences, paving the way for me to see myself as a powerful woman worthy of the love of a great man.

Considering the strength of our union and all we endured together, the notion of a pretty young thing at the office stealing Michael away seemed ludicrous. I knew he loved me just as much as I loved him and neither one of us wanted to mess that up. Despite our rock-solid bond, the monster still sneaks out every once in a while. My jealousy can even flair up when he drools over such cinematic "threats" as Halle Barry or Catherine Zeta-Jones. Not coincidentally, these moments of fear and insecurity tend to surface when I am ungrounded, feeling overwhelmed, taking inadequate care of myself, or riding the hormonal roller coaster. During these vulnerable moments my hot husband responds as he always has: he smiles sweetly, holds me close, tells me he loves me, and assures me that I am still, and always will be, the perfect woman for him. I must have done something pretty freakin' good in a past life to deserve this guy...

TO VIBE
OR NOT TO VIBE

I RECENTLY LEARNED that all vibrators are *not* created equal. I have employed a generic all-purpose vibrator for over fifteen years, and she has more than earned the nickname "Ol' Reliable". She may not have all the bells and whistles of the fancy new toys, but she gets the job done simply and quickly each and every time. Her task is simple: make Mama moan.

One afternoon I found myself in a creative funk. I wouldn't call it writer's block, but it was definitely a case of writer's speedbump. Preoccupied with several other issues, I was experiencing my first bout of literary constipation. I tried the usual methods to get my creative juices flowing such as meditation, yoga, playing the piano, and dancing; none were effective. It seemed that if I wanted the words to come, then I had to first. This was clearly a job for Ol' Reliable. After a blissful unaccompanied quickie, I was able to crank out a tasty literary morsel contained somewhere within these pages.

Despite Ol' Reliable's proven track record for creating pleasure and releasing tension, it was starting to become obvious that she was getting tired of the grind. The old girl was on her last C batteries and was literally screeching to be put down. If I wanted to meet my deadlines, I would soon need to find a permanent replacement for my handheld buddy.

I recalled several girlfriends waxing enthusiastic about something called a 'Rabbit'. This particular brand of vibrator has a reputation for outstanding orgasmic facilitation. I deserve a quality masturbatory experience just like the next gal, so I decided to check out this engineering masterpiece. One day while alone in the house, I blushingly googled "Rabbit". Lo and behold, the fifth entry on the list was the plastic, furless, mechanical bunny I was looking for. Within five minutes I had made my choice, opting for the cute pink Pearl model apparently ideal for beginners.

Finally the blessed day arrived. The Rabbit was delivered to my doorstep wrapped in its discreet packaging. As I looked at the innocuous box I wondered if the folks at the post office knew that a sexual naughty was inside. Were there special markings on the package that screamed "PERVERT!" in Postalese? Whether I had been found out or not, I wasn't about to waste any more time; I had to discover the magic enclosed within the bubble wrap. Mama had just received a brand new toy and was dying to play with it.

After experimenting with the Rabbit's dizzying array of speeds and positions, I finally found my groove. Boy, oh boy, did I find my groove! There's one word that came to mind after reaching the end zone with the help of my new pink pet: Wow. WOW! WOW!! I had no idea that masturbation could be that good. WOW. My challenge with the Rabbit wasn't going to be if I liked her or not, it would be avoiding carpel tunnel syndrome from overuse. Still, I've never been a daily diddler and didn't want to become one now. (I'm busy enough as it is.) So I am treating the Rabbit more like a piece of gourmet, organic dark chocolate—having her every once in a while is absolutely wonderful, but a steady diet would undoubtedly cause breakouts.

My dirty little secret isn't that I have a vibrator; it's that I have used one over the last ten years unbeknownst to my husband.

Hmmm...I guess he knows now. I have been secretly playing solo for years without mentioning this little factoid to my dearest beloved. I've shared many secrets with him over the course of our marriage, but this one I have kept carefully hidden. Why is masturbation different than all of the other nasties I've been able to own up to?

My reticence to claim my vibratory power was born out of Western society's puritanical view of sexuality. I grew up in the pre-"Sex and the City" era where masturbation was considered shameful and absolutely verboten. Since I was not raised in an overly strict household I was mercifully spared the 'go blind, then go to hell' teachings at home; however, I received similar messages through school, books, television, and movies. The fear of being seen as a twisted nympho kept me from fessing up to my 'sin of the flesh', even to the love of my life.

I am dumbfounded when I think about how most of us were made to feel guilty for having committed this natural act. By its simplest definition, masturbation is the act of pleasuring oneself. How have legions of people been brainwashed into thinking that feeling good is bad? What is wrong with pleasure? What is wrong with our bodies? What is wrong with releasing pent-up physical energy so one can be more vibrant, balanced, and creative? Can someone please tell me how experiencing delicious tinglies at our own hands detracts from the love we have for our partners or the devotion we have to Spirit? I just don't get it.

I've decided to proudly proclaim my practice of masturbation. I love my body, dammit, and will no longer be ashamed to enjoy it. My body adores making love to my husband, but it also derives intense satisfaction from dancing, receiving bodywork, practicing yoga, floating in the pool on a sunny day, and yes, diddling. Pleasures of the body are a Divine birthright, even if they sometimes require batteries to get us there.

In Defense
of Scheduling Sex

I BELIEVE IN SCHEDULING SEX. I know this may brand me as an unromantic bore, but trust me, there is a method to my blandness. Before I present my case for putting copulation on the calendar, I must clarify for whom this suggestion does not apply. If you are having wild, spontaneous and abundant rolls in the hay you may disregard this sage advice for the time being. I can only assume that you are one of the following: a) in that young, single, and sex-crazed phase of your life, b) in a new relationship that is intoxicatingly passionate, c) don't have a job, kids, or pets, or d) an alien. If you chose a, b, or c, it would be prudent to dog-ear this page for future reference. You will thank me for it later when you no longer have impromptu sexual liaisons on the kitchen counter. For the rest of you, if you want mind-blowing sex with your partner, take it from me—start putting it in your Blackberry.

Let's face it, sex in long-term relationships changes over time. At the beginning, your body aches for your lover's touch. After several years, the ache you feel is confined solely to your head. For most couples the frequency slowly changes from thrice-daily to thrice-weekly to thrice-monthly to once every lunar eclipse. When

I first got married a friend mentioned that she and her husband scheduled "date nights" each week to have sex. I relayed this little piece of matrimonial advice to Michael while entwined in one of our blissful, post-coital Saturday afternoon cuddles. We both had a big laugh at how pathetic it was to preplan lovemaking. We would *never* need to schedule sex in our marriage! Fast forward ten years and one child later, and every Sunday night in the Rose household is officially "Mom and Dad Time".

Why did we make the decision to earmark one night a week for our carnal pursuits? Because life happens. Daily activities take longer than the hours available to perform them. We wake up at a quarter-to-nothing every morning to start our litany of tasks: meditate, exercise, make breakfasts, pack lunches, iron shirts, take showers, get dressed, and drop Emma off at school. Then, after busting our butts all day at work, we come home and face the evening chores: make dinner, do dishes, schlep Emma to Karate class or piano lessons, get baths taken, clean the house, do laundry, and shop for groceries. At the end of most days, we are both exhausted and the notion of nookie is far from either of our minds. We usually have enough energy to read for ten minutes and then it's lights-out.

In this state of perpetual busyness, our "lower priority" items like sex sometimes got postponed or ignored altogether. During periods of accidental celibacy we became distant, selfish, and snippy with each other. Since we don't live in a vacuum, our quiet unhappiness impacted our daughter, other family and friends, co-workers, and anyone else who was unfortunate enough to cross our paths. At one point this got to be a *big* problem. We realized that our vanishing intimacy struck at the very core of our union and jeopardized our marriage.

Michael and I hated the emotional ups and downs that resulted from our waning sex life. To sustain a healthy and happy marriage, intimacy could no longer be perceived as a low priority item. We eventually woke up from our marital sleepwalking after discovering the ancient art of Tantra. Contrary to what some people believe,

Tantra isn't about having weird, unnatural sex for hours on end or turning oneself into a human pretzel. Instead, Tantra is a spiritual practice where one perceives the Divine in everything, especially one's lover. It is about establishing ritual and bringing sacredness into lovemaking. It is honoring sex as a pathway to Spirit. It is a glorious and powerful moving meditation. In short, Tantra is the antithesis of the "wham, bam, thank you ma'am" kind of sex most of us learned. Practicing sacred sexuality taught us to stop *having sex* (as if we owned it) and to start *making love* (like making gooey chocolate-chip cookies only much, much more fun).

Through this new lens Michael and I openly discussed every element of our sex life. We talked about how we wanted more out of our marriage than just friendly cohabitation. We shared our deepest sexual fears and traumas in a judgment-free cocoon of trust. We talked about our preconceptions of what sex *should* be and how we could be more creative in the bedroom. Finally, we talked logistics. With our busy lives how would we find the time and energy to regularly practice sacred sex? The answer was simple—schedule it.

Thanks to our weekly date night my husband and I are closer, happier and friskier than ever before. Sunday afternoons often include a brief catnap for each of us so we have enough energy for our special evening. After our naps, we finish up the remaining family activities and start getting into an amorous frame of mind. Once our darling daughter goes to bed we light candles, burn incense, put on soft music and lock the bedroom door. Our weekly journey to sexual ecstasy begins.

The impact of our date nights goes well beyond Sunday evening's physical pleasures. Our commitment to Tantric practice has strengthened our relationship immeasurably through honesty and openness. More than the earth-shattering orgasms that accompany conscious lovemaking (and believe me darlin', they *are* earth-shattering), it is the deepening emotional connection that is the true payoff.

Of course one has to adopt an attitude of flexibility even with the best-laid plans. Sometimes the mood for love strikes us outside of sacred Sundays, and we certainly don't abstain because it's the wrong day. Nor are we above the occasional quickie in the wee hours of the morning. But even with these lighter trips to Hornyville, our sexual practice has taught us to honor each other's feelings. We don't do the horizontal tango unless both of us are emotionally present and accounted for. I have heard too many horror stories from women who feel like their husbands' prostitutes. Obligatory sex where one person feels like a service provider is distasteful at best and cause for infidelity or divorce at worst.

In conclusion, if you and your partner want to feel like true lovers, either for the first time or once again, consider allocating one morning, afternoon, or evening a week to honor each other in conscious sexual union. You'll both feel energized, sexy, focused, and rarin' to go. When you can be fully present with your mate, your hearts become full of love and your bodies full of heat. With that, I rest my case.

Taming the Beast

❧

I HATE IT WHEN MICHAEL AND I FIGHT. Thankfully our arguments are rare and mercifully brief. But what they lack in frequency and duration, they sure make up for in intensity. During the heat of our conflicts my dear husband typically and rather annoyingly remains perfectly calm and rational, whereas I regularly abandon my conscious mind and morph into Theresa the Evil Hosebeast. My combat-ready alter ego has acquired extraordinary superpowers—she can grow razor-sharp fangs, shoot fire out of her eyes, spew poison with her words, and create an impenetrable force field around her.

The other day Michael and I had such a fight, and as if right on cue, the Evil Hosebeast appeared armed with verbal venom, angry tears, and the ever-popular protracted silent treatment. As with nearly all of our disagreements the genesis of this latest skirmish was my overreaction to something he said. Here's the Reader's Digest version: 1) I shared something very sensitive with Michael, 2) he didn't react in the way I wanted, and 3) I went ape-shit. In the interest of full disclosure, Michael's response would have been completely appropriate if he were having the discussion with any rational being. However, he *wasn't* talking to a rational being; he was talking to his crazy hormonal wife and the topic at hand was exercise and her weight. Poor man, he never even had a chance.

When Michael realized the hornet's nest he unwittingly got himself into, he swiftly apologized and told me exactly what I wanted to hear. For the rest of the day he was the model spouse—sweet, loving, attentive, and agreeable. Logic would dictate that our conflict end. However, despite my husband's admirable efforts, the fight remained very much alive within me. Throughout the day I had a ferocious scowl on my face, barked one-word answers to innocent questions, and basically was your standard nightmare. I tried several times to snap out of my bad mood, yet my anger and hurt kept holding on.

As I lay crying in bed later that night, clarity eventually enveloped me like a welcome breeze. I realized that growing up in an alcoholic family caused me to frequently feel unsafe, both emotionally and physically. To protect myself during those fearful moments I split in two: the Real Me and the Wounded Me. The Real Me is the person within who feels, loves, thinks, and honestly communicates. She is the conscious part of me. The Wounded Me is the little girl who shuts up, shuts down, runs away, and tries to become invisible. She is also known to become a human volcano exploding her anger randomly in all directions. She is the unhealed, unconscious part of me. When I am in an emotionally unsafe environment, as I felt I was earlier in the day, the Real Me essentially leaves my body and lets the wounded part take over. The Wounded Me does her job very well, employing any and all protective measures until she feels it is safe for the Real Me to return.

With the covers over my head I became aware of my physical self: a pounding headache, bloodshot eyes, runny nose, and unhappy heart. This wasn't fun for anyone, and I desperately wanted to reach the true end of the argument. I found it very difficult to put aside my anger and show my vulnerability; I didn't want to tell Michael what I *really* needed. Despite my desire to stay buried underneath the blankets, I summoned the courage to get out of bed, wash my face, and share my feelings with the man I love.

I described how I protect myself during conflicts and once my shadow side assumes power, true resolution can't take place through logic, contrition, or even the most heartfelt apology. (Unsurprisingly, Michael seemed very familiar with this phenomenon!) I admitted that there's only one thing that will get this mighty beast to retreat into her netherworld—a good old-fashioned hug. It couldn't be your garden-variety, quick pat-on-the-back, one-second hug either. It needed to be a hug so powerful, so full of light and compassion that its love pierces my armor, seeps into my cells, and melts away my dark insecurities, making me safe once again.

My understanding husband responded to my admission in the best possible way—he simply wrapped his arms around me and tenderly held me until my hard heart softened, the beast departed, and the Real Me returned. Ahhh...at long last our fight was finally over! Indeed, loving touch is the most powerful salve for my wounded heart.

CHOICES HAVE
CONSEQUENCES

❧

SOMETHING HAD TO GIVE. When my mom got sick, I was overwhelmed with emotion, responsibilities and tasks. I had more on my plate than I could handle but didn't stop to acknowledge that fact or take steps to address it. I got to my breaking point and then sprinted right past it. As usual, I wanted so badly to be everything to everyone that I ignored the warning signs of impending danger.

In his typical Prince Charming fashion, Michael stepped up to the plate when I needed him. Since I was often at Mom's house, my husband graciously and selflessly took care of Emma and managed most of the household tasks in addition to working his stressful full-time job. Things were not easy for him, yet he kept handling all that was thrown his way with little or no complaint.

Naturally my focus was on my mother and spending as much of our remaining time together as possible. The rest of my non-Mom time was spent ensuring that my daughter, other family members, friends, clients, students, and staff were getting some attention. Everyone got a little piece of me—everyone but my husband. The one relationship I didn't think I needed to worry about—my marriage—was the one that suffered the most.

Michael and I had endured other difficult life events during our relationship including the passing of Michael's mother. After each ordeal we became closer and our bond grew stronger. Naturally, we expected the same from my mother's illness, but it turned out to be one of our toughest challenges, one that brought us dangerously close to the breaking point.

As Mom's death became imminent, things started getting really tense in our home. Michael and I were running on fumes and weren't going to "waste" energy on the one person we thought would always be there. Due to our mutual lack of attention there was no longer the "us" that we knew. Instead, there were just two unhappy, exhausted individuals tackling their respective responsibilities as best they could. Just as my mother's body was withering away, so was my marriage.

Our rock-solid union started to crumble when we stopped taking time to talk, listen, hug, goof around, and make love. Our brief conversations were usually limited to communicating status and confirming action items. Sometimes we'd perfunctorily ask each other how our days were, and mutter a "fine" in response when they were anything but. In a few short months we had regressed from passionate lovers to annoyed roommates.

Right after Mom's memorial we were barely speaking to each other. After returning home with my niece Briana from picking up Mom's ashes from the cremation society, Michael and I got into an enormous fight—the biggest, scariest one ever. Everything we hadn't said to each other over the last five months came exploding out of us as we angrily cursed and screamed at the other. It was at that tearful moment, nose-to-nose in rage and disappointment, when our marriage was facing the greatest threat to its survival. Blessedly, Briana was able to distract Emma from overhearing our verbal brawl (at least this is what I have convinced myself).

After seething in our own juices for a few days, the two of us simmered down enough to have a civilized conversation. Initially it was tempting to play the blame game and find fault in how the other behaved. But the simple truth was that we hated being this miserable and wanted to find our way back to bliss again. So, calmly and without judgment, we conducted a post-mortem of The Tragic Rose Debacle of 2006.

We reminded each other about one of our core philosophies: *choices have consequences*. We admitted that we *both* chose to put other things above our marriage, take the other person for granted, and stifle our feelings instead of openly sharing them. No one person was at fault. We both owned the mess we were in, and both of us suffered mightily the consequences: alienation, loneliness and resentment, to name but a few. Relationships, just like all living things, need attention or even the heartiest will die.

The pain and regret of that time has left a permanent mark on me. I am sad that we said those hurtful, angry words to each other. I am sad that the profound experience of witnessing my mother's conscious death wasn't fully shared with my partner. I am sad that I relied on others for nurturing and emotional support. I am sad that we both chose poorly over and over again.

Despite all that happened during those difficult months we knew our marriage was worth fighting for, and luckily the damage inflicted was not irreparable. Our hearts were wounded but not yet broken, and mending them required attention, compassion and time. Michael and I made a commitment to each other to give our union its much-needed care and feeding.

We admitted our poor choices and together, with courage and trust, released the judgment and anger we felt. We saw no point in holding grudges, rehashing mistakes or assigning blame. We breathed life back into our marriage with more talking and less silence; more lovemaking and less TV; more gratitude and less entitlement. We just paid more attention to each other. Through these simple acts, the "us" eventually returned.

Since our voyage to the precipice, Michael and I value each other more than ever before and vow to honestly express our feelings regardless of the circumstance. Even though it was the most heart-wrenching time in my life, traveling through that dark night of my soul had a precious gift buried beneath it. I was painfully yet thoroughly reminded of how much I love that man.

RAISING KIDS

"If you bungle raising your children, I don't think whatever
else you do well matters very much."

—Jacqueline Kennedy Onassis

FETAL WISDOM

CB

MY DAUGHTER first contradicted me at thirty-seven weeks in utero. At issue were the particulars of her arrival. We wanted *au natural* but she opted for high-tech.

When Michael and I found out I was pregnant, we began researching all of the birthing options available. As quasi-hippies we decided on a midwife-assisted natural delivery at a birthing center. Most of the materials we read waxed poetic about natural childbirth, and we became enthralled with the idea of a water birth. I spent many a night visualizing the serenity and sacredness of plopping Emma into a warm bathtub surrounded by candles, soft music, and smiling faces. There was just one teensy little problem: Emma had decided otherwise.

During my third trimester we learned that the baby's position is critical to receiving the go-ahead for a water birth. If Emma was going to take the typical exit door out of my womb, her little noggin would need to be pointing downward. We were advised that if Emma's head was in any other place at the time of the Big Push, a water birth or any other form of natural birth would be risky for both of us. Throughout my pregnancy Emma twirled around so much that I could barely keep track of which lump was her head and which was her rump. Michael and I nicknamed her "The Bean" because she seemed to be hopping around inside me like a Mexican jumping bean. With a child this adventurous there would be no problem when the big day arrived. Or so I thought.

About three weeks before her due date, Emma abruptly stopped her dancing and struck her favorite pose: sitting on my pelvic floor with her head wedged underneath my right rib cage. (Knowing my daughter she was probably already practicing the full lotus yoga posture.) My midwife, Heidi, started to voice concerns about Emma's position, informing me that my little bundle would need to do a 180° turn pretty soon or my tranquil birthing center vision would be replaced with an operating room at the local hospital. Heidi cheerfully told me that I had plenty of time to coax Emma into the starting gate and gave me all sorts of alternative strategies to facilitate my daughter's final spin.

For the next few weeks I did everything humanly possible to get that kid heading south. I meditated while lying in an inverted position, I had Michael talk to her while he rested his cheek on my pubic bone, I received acupressure and moxibustion, I got special chiropractic treatments, I took homeopathic medicine, I placed a walkman playing classical music onto my lower abdomen, and I even did cartwheels in the pool every day. (Thank goodness there are no visual recordings of my Mary Lou Retton aqua routines.) Every last repositioning remedy was unsuccessful.

As a final Hail Mary, I submitted to the excruciatingly painful medical procedure called external cephalic version. This is a process whereby an obstetrician *manually* turns the baby an inch at a time. After what seemed like hours of experiencing the most wretched pain imaginable, the doctor finally finished the medieval torture. With all of that poking and prodding Emma actually ended up in the desired location!

I was so relieved I was going to be able to move forward with my original birth plan that I almost, *almost*, forgot about the agonizing pain in my uterus. Alas, The Bean had the last word. Within just a few hours of the procedure, I could feel her doing the electric boogaloo in my womb, returning to her favorite nook by the end of the day. The only difference was that we were a little poorer and I was a whole lot sorer.

Despite our attempts at a natural birth I ended up delivering Emma via C-section in a cold, harsh operating room complete with a double epidural. After forty-five minutes of Dr. What's-His-Name yanking on her, The Bean finally relented and left her safe, cozy confines. Immediately after her departure, she experienced a brief instance of respiratory distress where she wasn't breathing. I will never forget the agony of waiting to hear my child's cry while the nurses vainly tried to distract us from the silence. Thankfully, a few moments later, we heard the magnificent sound of her little squeak.

The birth vision of my dreams, blissful in its perfection, was a far cry from what I actually experienced. Rather than participating in a sacred and profound rite of passage, I endured a difficult surgery in the bright lights of an operating room. My nurses were cranky, my recovery room was cold and dirty, and I wasn't able to hold my newborn until more than an hour after she was taken out of me. I was so angry with the hospital staff that I forced them to discharge me less than two days after my surgery so we could recover in peace at home.

For years I have held on to the anger of that day. I still feel pangs of regret for not bringing my angel into the world with more peace, love, and Spirit. On the other hand, I cannot help but be grateful that modern medical technology enabled me to deliver her safely. Had we moved forward with our original plans, the breech delivery may have caused complications, and God forbid, something might have happened to Emma. Candles, music and bathtubs seem pretty freakin' insignificant compared to the life and health of my little girl.

As I work to let go of the birth trauma that both of us endured, I am now choosing to believe that Emma understood my internal terrain better than anyone else. She was *in* my womb for over nine months and knew what things were like in there. Maybe Emma recognized that the only successful exit strategy was the one where she would be pulled through a hole cut in her mama's belly. By adopting this larger perspective I can finally stop cursing my C-section and its corresponding unpleasantries. Instead, I will now choose to honor my scar, my sagging gut, and our remarkable experience of July 9, 2001 as the first of many profound examples of my daughter's independence and infinite wisdom.

HAVING A BABY:
NO ASSEMBLY REQUIRED

I WAS NEVER ONE to do anything half-assed. When I became pregnant six years ago, I took on motherhood with incredible focus, dedication, and perhaps a wee bit of obsession. I devoured every baby book I could lay my hands on, read every parenting magazine cover to cover, and surfed a multitude of pregnancy web sites so as to commit their FAQs to memory. I had no clue about the complexities of modern maternity until I started reading these publications. How did zillions of women throughout the ages deliver healthy babies without knowing what to expect when they're expecting?

The more information I absorbed, the greater my anxiety levels became. I started to think that in order to thoroughly evaluate, procure and assemble the required supplies and equipment I would need to devote myself to the project full-time. To provide the most basic needs for my child, both in and out of the womb, I would clearly need a leave of absence from my job. If only I could have convinced my husband of the critical nature of my task. Imagine the spousal cruelty: being forced to continue working instead of reading pregnancy books all day!

Nevertheless, I somehow found time for my fetal fixation. I allocated nearly every spare moment to researching the foods I should and shouldn't eat, what music I should and shouldn't listen to, how to breathe properly, and scads of other mission-critical items. (Note to all expectant mothers: If you dare to consume a single portion of deli meat, soft cheese, or God forbid, canned tuna, your child will most likely be born with two heads. You've been warned.)

I endlessly analyzed the developmental chart taped to our refrigerator and obsessed over pregnancy milestones. I would consult the chart several times a week to confirm if my current weight gain was in the normal range, if my little punkin' had sprouted fingers and toes yet, or how many kicks to expect per hour. But by far the biggest energetic abyss I fell into during my pregnancy was the laborious process of identifying and acquiring the appropriate baby gear.

It shames me to admit how much useless crap my husband and I purchased. We spent hundreds of dollars on stuff, stuff and more stuff. In the name of providing only the "essential" things for our little EmmaBean, we acquired two types of strollers, three different car seats, swings, jumpers, bouncy seats, travel playpens, activity centers, three portable potties, Baby Bjorns, Boppies, musical mobiles, and a staggering collection of loud, brightly-colored toys, all allegedly designed to foster our baby's Inner Mozart and/or Einstein.

With a cornucopia of toys, machines and other necessaries at her disposal, what was our daughter's favorite activity? Lying on her belly on our tile floor swooshing her arms and legs back and forth like a salamander; we even nicknamed her "The Tile Swimmer". Alas, the source of true kiddie bliss required no assembly or D batteries. Had Michael and I known this before buying half the items on our must-have list, we would have saved ourselves a buttload of time, money, and energy.

From my sincere desire to be the best mom possible and have a happy, safe child, no expense seemed too great nor any item too silly. All I can say in my defense is that I was hoodwinked. Brain-washed. Bamboozled. Sold a bill of goods. I essentially took leave of my senses when I plugged into the marketing machine known as having a baby in the webified 21st Century. My overriding impression from the web sites and books I read was that I *had* to purchase the latest and greatest gadgets or risk my child's bodily harm, emotional scarring or mental retardation.

My mom used to tease me about my anal-retentive approach to the whole baby thing. Whenever I'd start freaking out that I wasn't doing something "right", she would remind me that when she was pregnant with me, she smoked cigarettes like a chimney, ate whatever she wanted, and sucked down coffee, wine, and Pepsi with utter abandon. This was on top of putting me in the front seat of the car without so much as a seat belt, much less strapped into the NASA-approved five-point harness car seat with a LATCH anchor system, infant headrest and ergonomic carrying handle. She'd always finish her rant by saying, "and you turned out all right!" Frightening, but true.

In hindsight I see that the vast majority of the gear was not purchased in our best interest but for those of the various stores and manufacturers. My voracious appetite for more and more baby data didn't make me a better mommy, it just made me a more jittery one. Ultimately, the only thing that ever really mattered was the boundless love the three of us shared—that and keeping my job so I could help pay for all of that junk.

The Siren's Call of Pacifiers, TV and EasyMac

A N OVERWORKED, EXHAUSTED MOTHER must have invented the pacifier, a rubber nipple-shaped piece of sublime ingenuity. This parenting doohickey was aptly named as it so brilliantly quiets the savage beast known as the cranky baby. I was given a pacifier when I was an infant, and my entire family deferentially referred to it as "the Bink". Apparently every time I eked out so much as a whimper my four-year old brother Doug would implore anyone within earshot to "Get the Bink! Get the Bink!" Whoever was the first responder would quickly pop the plastic nipple into my mouth, thus silencing any utterances of displeasure. The cycle was simple: baby cries, baby gets plastic in mouth, baby quiets down. All quiet on the Midwestern front.

Yet somewhere between 1969 and 2001 the pacifier became passé. People discovered that pacifiers were causing tooth misalignment, were repositories for all sorts of disgusting germs, and brought with them an eventual weaning process nearly tantamount to kicking a nasty heroin habit. By the time I had my own baby, I understood that using a pacifier was a big fat no-no among the overly obsessive mommies-to-be crowd, of which I was one.

After Emma was born, I experienced previously unknown depths of physical and mental exhaustion due to my juggling act of being a first-time mother, working a stressful corporate job, finishing my college degree and moving into a new home. Despite my valiant attempts to adhere to all of the rules of perfect mommyhood, I eventually succumbed to The Dark Side and bowed to the power of the Bink. Somehow by the grace of God, Emma avoided a full-blown addiction to the Bink, mercifully establishing a relatively brief union with it. I do, however, recall taking several airplane flights with my child in tow where her cherubic mouth was firmly corked from departure to arrival.

Six years later I have reluctantly employed a whole new generation of quasi-pacifiers in an effort to make our lives simpler, quieter, and generally more enjoyable. These pacifiers aren't considered to be the most ideal of parenting tactics, but they are fixtures in my world nonetheless. I have long since surrendered the fantasy of a "No TV, No Sugar" household. Emma's Bink Version 2.0 contains frequent DVD viewings, macaroni and cheese consumption, visits to Noggin.com, and road trips to the drive-thru at Dairy Queen. My daughter has even had bowls of Honey Nut Cheerios—for dinner.

I suppose there are those rare mothers out there who have somehow managed to run an electronics-free home, make healthy meals and snacks, play educational games and read with their children every single day, have a successful career, keep the house clean, maintain a thriving marriage, and create a modicum of time for their own pleasurable pursuits, all without medicating themselves. I'm just not one of them. Sure, I'd like to be the holistic June Cleaver of the 21st Century, but frankly I don't have the energy for it.

I'm not proud to admit this, but sometimes I just need a little break from my six-year old. Emma is like so many other children in that she has two speeds in which she operates: full throttle and stop. At her age she doesn't understand the nuances of a mid-afternoon lull in energy; she just wants to run, play and talk, *all of the time.* Being more than thirty years her senior, I simply can't keep up with her pace. When I push myself beyond what feels natural and reasonable, I inevitably end up getting snippy, losing my patience about something silly, and ultimately ruining a perfectly good day. I've made this mistake far too many times, and I don't like how it feels for any of us. So when I reach the end of my rope, I reach for the remote. Emma can boob-out for an hour and a half watching *Thumbelina* for the bazillionth time, and I can crash in bed for a much-needed and well-deserved nap. Everybody wins.

Yet these tranquil moments often precede a self-inflicted emotional backlash. I'd incessantly second-guess all of my parental choices involving TV and sugar, harshly judging them against some wacky ideal of the perfect mom. Is Emma watching too many movies? Is she eating too many sweets? Will she get some rare vitamin-deficiency disease from the lack of vegetables in her diet? Does she resent me for sending her to her room too often? Am I causing her irreparable emotional trauma?

On one hand I could rationalize I was doing a good job of parenting because Emma watches only recorded videos instead of broadcast television. She isn't exposed to the hypnotic slew of commercials, thus sparing us the requests for Chocolate-covered Sugar Balls, the Barbie Super McMansion and other worthless merchandise. On the other hand I could argue that I was doing a bad job of parenting because Emma has watched umpteen movies over the years, has eaten a fair amount of cookies and ice cream, and could recite every *Ramona the Brave* audiobook by heart. It's true that children are affected by the foods they eat and the intellectual and visual stimulation they receive, but ultimately, if a child is consistently nurtured, listened to, supported, and loved-up, the grams of sugar ingested or hours of television watched are just not that important.

I have learned that I don't need to judge parents who choose to allow their children to watch TV every night, nor do I need to judge myself for letting my child watch a few DVDs on the weekend. Parenting, like life itself, is just a series of choices. Some of the choices we make are conscious, and some are not. Some are ideal, and some are not. They cannot be categorized as right or wrong because there is no definitive Book of Truth from which to evaluate. I am coming to realize that our choices as parents aren't good or bad; they just *are*. Given this awareness, I now try to make my parenting decisions based on my own inner voice instead of trying to attain the unattainable. I am dispelling the myth of the SuperMom. In my home, everyone is so much happier since I've given both Emma and myself permission not to be perfect, but just to *be*.

For years Michael and I have said goodnight to our daughter in the same way every single evening. We each get a chance to say two things that we will dream about. The dreams of our little EmmaBean have never ceased to disappoint, as they so often contain wisdom and gratitude that only a joyful child could deliver. A recent first dream of hers was "The power of God's healing" and the second was "My new glitter wand". Emma's words clearly demonstrated that she not only understands the importance of spirituality but also thoroughly embraces the entertaining, carnival-like physical aspect of life. As I look into my daughter's stunning green eyes and witness the journey of this amazing, happy, and loving being, I know that every single one of us has made some pretty darn good choices so far, all things considered. On that happy note, chocolate milk for everyone!

SLAYING THE BOGEYMAN

AFTER SIX YEARS as a parent I am officially putting The Bogeyman on notice. I finally see you for what you are, you vile beast, and I am no longer going to be your helpless victim.

The Bogeyman has been present from the moment my at-home pregnancy test came back positive until very recently. He has been a formidable foe, assuming a variety of identities and knowing exactly how to execute his ruthless assault when I am at my most vulnerable. He has been bigger than life yet can lurk in the darkest, quietest shadows of my being. He has been nastier and more destructive than anything I have ever faced. This supervillain goes by another name: *fear.*

He first appeared early in my pregnancy as I began my crash course in parentology. Never one to embark on anything in an ill-prepared fashion, I began assembling my study materials from copious parenting resources. I quickly learned that The Bogeyman lived on nearly every page I read, imprinting my psyche with the litany of ways my baby could be harmed during her stay in my uterus.

The literature contained stern warnings not to tell anyone about our wonderful news that we were expecting until after the twelfth week, as I had a 25% chance of miscarrying. Thus I experienced my first three months of pregnancy in a constant state of fear that I would surely become one of the tragic 25%. Additionally, thanks to my research, I could recite all of the reasons why delivering via Caesarian section was potentially harmful and traumatic for the baby. This information provided me no end of comfort when I was wheeled into the operating room to deliver Emma in that same manner. Ever the source of useful facts and helpful hints, those periodicals also taught me about sore nipple prevention, mucus plugs, episiotomies and other charming facets of childbirth.

Despite all of the worst-case scenarios to which I was exposed, Emma Nicole Rose safely entered the world in the summer of 2001. However, The Bogeyman quickly found new ways to spread his emotional poison back home. This time he took the form of "child safety precautions". As I did with my pregnancy, I became fluent in all of the potential dangers lurking around every corner of the house and the corresponding products that would help combat them.

The more I read the more I began to feel that no place was safe. Clearly, Michael and I needed to adopt a constant vigilance posture if we were to avoid our child's permanent scarring or God forbid, her untimely demise. At my frantic behest, Michael installed dozens of safety devices throughout the house, including but certainly not limited to hallway gates, outlet plugs, corner guards, cabinet and door locks, faucet covers, and the all-important toilet seat lock. We also created an interesting interior design motif where all objects were at least four feet above ground so our adventurous tot couldn't get her hands on *anything*. The pièce-de-résistance was the massive cage we had installed around our pool to prevent accidental drowning.

I hoped all of our efforts would at least mitigate, if not eliminate, the presence of The Bogeyman. If we just installed one more piece of equipment or removed one more potential hazard, our darling baby would be safe. Alas, The Bogeyman had a cruelly simple counterattack that would undercut all of my obsessive precautions: SIDS, Sudden Infant Death Syndrome. Even the name itself evokes dread in every parent simply because it is random, inexplicable, and totally out of one's control. Every morning I heard my daughter coo into the baby monitor was one more night we eluded the SIDS Monster.

Fear for my daughter's well-being has been silently running in the back of my mind for six long years. Ever the cunning adversary, The Bogeyman has very successfully co-opted the media in his effort to keep me constantly on edge and fearing the worst. Thanks to the media's fascination with the macabre, I have seen the ghastly news segments and movie trailers involving our little ones—tales of disfiguring injuries, terminal diseases, abuse, abduction, and murder. My fears grew exponentially larger a few years ago when Sam, my beautiful six-year old nephew, died from brain cancer. I was losing the war against The Bogeyman.

The battlefield abruptly changed last year when my mother got diagnosed with terminal cancer herself. One of the unexpected gifts of that experience was the quality time we had together frequently talking about our spiritual beliefs. We discussed the meaning of life, where we go when we die, and how everything, absolutely *everything*, happens exactly as it should in accordance with God's plan. The profound journey I took with Mom gave me crystal clarity on the nature of life and forever altered how I perceive the process of death.

I no longer have to fear that my child will die—because she will. So will I. So will you. So will every single human drawing a breath on this big rock called Earth. Like it or not that's the gig we all signed up for. It's not *if* Emma will leave this planet, but *when*. To be able to live each day with this awareness has required a new attitude on my part. Instead of cowering from The Bogeyman at every turn, I have decided to focus my energies toward believing that Emma will be here for as long as needed to serve her Divine Purpose, that Spirit is always watching out for her, and that whatever happens is in perfect alignment with her Highest Good. In essence I completely trust that God knows what He's (or She's) doing.

Don't get me wrong; I think trying to keep our children safe from harm is a good, responsible, and necessary thing every parent should do. I for one certainly don't want my daughter drinking Drano, juggling carving knives or playing in traffic. However, my husband and I have adopted a more reasonable, positive approach in helping to protect our daughter. It all boils down to fewer locks and cages, more communication and trust.

Unfortunately, The Bogeyman has not disappeared entirely. He can still rear his ugly head when Emma gets hurt or when I hear disturbing stories involving children. In those cases my greatest weapon is to become aware of the beast as quickly as possible, name him for what he really is, and slay him with my unwavering belief and trust in Spirit. Each day I try to be a mom that really, truly believes that all is well, all of the time.

BECAUSE I SAID SO

☙

I AM HORROR-STRUCK when I think of some of the things that have come out of my mouth when communicating with my daughter. I have shouted, screamed, barked, snarled, and otherwise spewed like a troll of mythic proportions. As a representative of all Troll-Parents who occasionally make abominable choices, I am here to admit the crimes against our offspring so we may begin to forgive ourselves just a little bit.

Parenting was easy when my daughter was a relatively immobile infant. Sure, her arrival required additional levels of effort: preparing formula bottles in the middle of the night, laundering piles of burp rags and onesies, and changing hundreds of poopy diapers, to name a few. Even so, Emma was a pretty low-maintenance cohabitant. We could put her in a bouncy seat and spend hours basking in her giggles. When she developed her verbal and motor skills, however, everything in our lives changed. We got back on the plane and said good-bye to Mr. Rourke and "Fantasy Island." The real-life parenting challenges had begun.

As a mom, my biggest test occurs early in the morning. When I am in the whirlwind of school-day preparations, I do my best to stay remotely sane. Despite my efforts to remain calm and joyful, there lives within me a tough-as-nails drill sergeant that frequently shouts rapid-fire instructions to my slow-moving daughter to get her ready for school on time. "Quit dilly-dallying!" has become my morning mantra. Oh Dear Lord, please help me. I have incorporated "dilly-dally" into my vocabulary.

I also cringe at remembrances of how I treated Emma when I have been exhausted or in a foul mood. At six years old, she just wants to hang out with her two favorite people in the whole world, her Mom and Dad. Bless her heart; the little peanut has not yet hit the parents-are-the-root-of-all-evil phase. Sometimes she just wants share my physical space, but I don't have the patience or energy to handle the vibe of a wound-up first grader. During those times I have been known to relegate her to her room just so I can be alone. She hasn't done anything wrong, yet I am quasi-punishing her because of my own inability stay peaceful, joyous and grounded. I know there are many other ways that parents could handle those situations more consciously; but when I'm tired, cranky, and not feeling myself, I can't for the life of me recognize the enlightened options much less execute them.

The one thing that currently drives me loco is the fact that Emma's room often resembles a post-apocalyptic Toys-R-Us. She loves to have a messy room and feels more comfortable in it. I, on the other hand, can't stand to have any part of our home look like Dorothy's house just before it drops on the witch. I know I can shut her door, but I don't want to have to. Hence, a major power struggle between mom and daughter unfolds. When I'm particularly obsessive about getting the house straightened-up, I have on more than one occasion thrown her playthings shouting, "This room looks like a pig sty!"

I've yelled, "Because I said so!", "Because I'm the parent, that's why!", and "None of your business!" when faced with a barrage of innocent questions. I've snapped, "I said no and I mean *no!*" in the middle of food negotiations. Worse than any of these parental power tools I have wielded is the cruelest response of all; I have completely ignored her.

I've slammed doors, thrown out favorite toys, sent her to bed without dinner, and left her crying in her bed without so much as a good-night much less a kiss on the forehead. I have screamed at her so loud that my throat burned and my head ached. I have never hit Emma, but I have felt angry enough to do so. Yes, all of this toxic poison has come out of me and been directed toward my beautiful daughter, and nearly all of it borne out of something utterly insignificant. Wow. What a colossal shit I am.

I have just illustrated in shocking detail the shame most parents feel when they consider the nasty things they sometimes do to their kids. As moms and dads we want so badly to do a better job than that of our parents, knowing how messed-up we got from some of the stupid stuff they did. We desperately want to break the cycle, yet we inevitably find ourselves screaming in the hallway every once in a while. Our kids bear the brunt of our weakness, fear, and anger because of the illusory power we have over them. Essentially we scream at them because we can.

At this point in my life it is an unrealistic goal to eliminate all instances of my unconscious, irrational parenting. The raving lunatic or hard-assed drill sergeant will undoubtedly rear her ugly head again. My real goal is to be aware of my interactions, understand my emotions and their root causes, and minimize my *Mommie Dearest* moments as much as possible.

The best thing I can do when I become the Troll-Mother-From-Hell is that which I have taught Emma to do whenever she makes a poor choice: have the courage to own it and do whatever it takes to make it right. Most often, the best way I can do so is to simply sit down with my wee sprite, wipe our tears away, and humbly apologize for hurting her feelings. I try not to make excuses or blame anyone else for my bad behavior. Instead, I just say what's in my heart. I tell her why I acted like a crazy woman and how very sorry I am.

No matter how you spin it, conscious parenting is hard work. There are days when we are the epitome of proper role modeling and days when we act like Joan Crawford with PMS. The best we can do is the best we can do, and we should cut ourselves some slack for being human. I can easily imagine sitting down with my daughter in a few decades, having tea and listening to horror stories of things she has said to my grandchildren. When that happens I'll reach over and gently touch Emma's hand, assuring her that I know *exactly* how she feels.

Growing Pains

THIS MORNING, for the first time, I nervously put my only child on the school bus. Emma woke up at 5:30 wildly excited about her newest adventure: starting first grade. She couldn't wait to be a part of the new campus, hang out with the older kids, tote her Tinkerbell backpack filled with big-kid school supplies, and, of course, ride the bus. Today marks a moment of change and growth for both of us.

My daughter's latest milestone hit me like a freight train. In an instant, Emma has shed her little girl-ness in favor of a new, big-girl identity. She now possesses a more scrutinizing eye for fashion, is mortified by the idea of pigtails in her hair, and is greatly concerned that the freckles on her cheeks will make her unattractive to the boys. She even went so far as to declare that pink was no longer her favorite color and she didn't like the Disney princesses anymore. (Hannah Montana has summarily replaced the animated divas as her new object of obsession.) I never thought I'd see the day when I actually felt melancholy at the thought of no more pink princess junk scattered around the house.

The facts are indisputable: Emma is growing up. Where did the time go? How did it happen so quickly? Now I realize why old folks always say, "It seems like just yesterday when you were a little baby." Because it really *does* seem like yesterday. One minute I was changing Em's diapers whilst singing about Elmo's world, and the next minute she's instructing me on the proper use of hair accessories.

As I said goodbye to Emma this morning, I felt an equal mix of pride and apprehension. Since she attends a Montessori school she'll be in a classroom with children up to nine years of age. She'll adore this new environment where she'll make lots of new friends, learn more about the world around her, and expand her already-freakish vocabulary. Speaking of vocabulary, the words 'hate', 'ugly', and 'stupid' are generally considered naughty ones in the Rose household. Now that she'll be with older kids, I imagine she'll probably learn a few new colorful alternatives.

I'm also not looking forward to those uncomfortable questions such as, "Mama, why does Brandon call his little sister a wanker?", "What is divorce and why do some parents get one?", or "How come Jessica doesn't believe in God?" These and many other touchy questions are what lie ahead. Given that we have never received the Parenting for Dummies manual, Michael and I will just have to take each issue as it comes, addressing them with as much grace and wisdom as we can muster.

It was a sad day when I realized my baby is no longer a baby. Emma's clothes, shoes, hair, music and toys all reflect her sprouting maturity. Yet I continue to hold on by my fingernails to the vision of her as a baby, and so far Emma is still indulging me. She continues to lovingly cuddle with her parents, give cubby bearhugs and heart-melting smooches, and allow us to wrap her in a towel and toss her on the bed after every bath. Knowing that these special moments won't last forever, I have mentally tattooed some of the most precious of the bunch. I hope I never forget the blissful feeling of gently rubbing my little angel's back to wake her in the morning.

As an already-proud mama, I will be thrilled to witness Emma-Bean evolve into a fabulous and confident young woman. My rational side knows that change is inevitable and good. I don't need, nor would I want, to have her stay a little girl forever. There's so much for her to share with the world! But even as I grow accustomed to this unfolding, I still wouldn't say no to another decade or so of unbridled cuddling. Even after the fantasy decade comes to a close and she traipses off to the delightful land of womanhood, I will find comfort in knowing that my dear, sweet Emma will always be my baby.

DIARY OF A MAD
FIRST GRADER

I COMMITTED A CARDINAL SIN this morning—I read my daughter's diary. Given that Emma is just learning to write, I assumed I wouldn't find anything too shocking. However, a picture is worth a thousand words, and I discovered that a Hello Kitty sticker is worth at least that much. Don't be fooled; that cute little white kitten can shoot daggers into your soul.

Emma received her coveted Hello Kitty diary for her sixth birthday. It's pink, fuzzy, and has the cheeky little feline printed on every page. The diary also contains stickers of Hello Kitty expressing various emotional states such as relaxed, happy, grumpy, angry, and playful. This is a feat in and of itself given that Miss Kitty has teeny black dots for eyes and no mouth whatsoever. To inspire the youthful diarist, each page is printed with "Today I am Feeling...", prompting my little darling to record her daily emotions through written word and/or sticker.

This morning as I was tidying-up the house I entered Emma's room in my typical self-deceptive manner: I began cleaning her room without admitting to myself I was cleaning it. Today's act of denial involved hanging up her wet towel from last night's bath, tossing all manner of dirty clothes into her hamper, returning drinking glasses to the kitchen, and straightening her comforter in order to simulate the rare image of an actual made bed. As I was about to leave Emma's room for the next puttering exercise, I spotted the diary.

I briefly skimmed through the first few pages hoping to sneak a quick peek into what I imagined would be my daughter's idyllic world. Instead I was shocked to see that most of the entries were not written in the usual pastel colored pencils of which Emma is so fond. Rather, most of the entries were angrily recorded in dark ink, clearly penned by an unhappy scribe. The words jumped off the page: "MAD!", "SAD!", "BAD!" and "FRUSTRATID!". Whoa! Did she really feel this awful? Driving the knife deeper into my heart, Emma had chosen Hello Kitty stickers that perfectly corresponded to her upset of the day. There was that damn cat giving me looks of anger and pain.

As I turned each page I kept holding on to the hope that the next entry would have a sunnier disposition. However, after perusing several pages it became clear that most contained unhappy words and cat-faces. Plopping down pitifully on Emma's princess bed, I felt like a shoo-in for the "Worst Mommy of the Year" award. How could my little darling have so much sadness in her? Was having me as a mother that terrible? How had I failed her? After spinning in the self-loathing cycle for several minutes, I finally stepped out of my own ego drama and began to see the situation more clearly.

I set aside my fixation on the diary contents for a moment and started to think about Emma herself. Anyone familiar with her knows that she's a happy child—a *really* happy child. She spreads truckloads of joy to others with her highly-contagious smile and exuberant manner. She has a belly-laugh that rattles the walls, and often spontaneously breaks into song. In short, Emma totally digs her life.

After regaining most of my mental faculties, I also considered how the diary actually serves Emma as an outlet to express her feelings. I fondly recalled my own diary and the critical role it played in my childhood. My most private and often saddest thoughts that couldn't or wouldn't be shared with anyone were nestled within the lined pages of my sacred red diary, safely protected by its tiny lock and key. How ironic it was for a writer to find fault with her child using the written word to express her feelings. Duh!

No doubt about it, Emma is a healthy, joyful, and well-adjusted child. But she is also human, and like the rest of us, she has mad, bad, sad and frustrated days. Actively encouraging my little one to process her feelings through writing and other creative expression will undoubtedly serve her for years to come. Rather than obsessing about my daughter's rare bad moods, I am opting to bask in the richness of her frequent bliss.

As if Divinely guided, I decided to take one final peek into Em's diary. The last page included a smiley face sticker, a beautiful pink hand-drawn heart, and one carefully printed word that encapsulates her outlook on life as well as the impact this little book of secrets has on it—"POSITIV". With that, I carefully placed the tiny diary back on her desk and happily continued my puttering.

MY GREATEST TEACHER

I FEEL LIKE I LIVE WITH YODA. Emma is our own Jedi Knight, small in stature but enormous in power and wisdom. On the surface our daughter is a typical first-grader: unlimited physical energy, nonstop verbal communication, and curious as the little monkey named George she loved so much as a toddler. However, when I observe her with my energy eyes I see much more than a little person who loves playing dress-up and eating macaroni & cheese. I see one of my greatest teachers.

Sadly, I sometimes catch myself minimizing Emma's energetic role in our family. I subconsciously convince myself that, because she is physically small without "important" responsibilities like a job or a marriage, she is somehow less of a contributor. However, when I tune into her as an expression of the Divine, I see her as so much more than my daughter; she is a powerful guide and a mirror through which I gain greater understanding of my own life.

Here is a typical lesson plan from my six-year old professor:

- Emma will show me when I am ungrounded or have become too absorbed with trivial things. When Michael and I observe recurring misbehavior in Emma, she is trying to show us that we are not listening to her need for nurturing or our own need for peace and connectedness to Spirit. We have found that the surest way to end a spell of misbehavior with Emma is to increase time spent meditating, exercising, reading, playing games, or just enjoying each other's company. Not only does Emma respond positively to these activities, but Michael and I also move to a more tranquil state of being.

- Emma lives each day with passion and enthusiasm. She can get blissed-out from dancing in the kitchen, singing in the car, riding her bicycle, or taking a bath. She doesn't wait for big moments to experience profound joy; her life is one long series of incredible moments, each worth savoring. When I see her face beaming from these simple activities, it gives me pause to review the daily events of my own life and see where I can put more happiness into them.

- Emma is integrated with Mother Nature. Thanks to her father's regular walks with her, Emma is fearless about nature and loves to explore. She derives immeasurable physical, emotional, and spiritual benefit from her nature expeditions, and she is growing up with a deep appreciation of the value and beauty of the Earth. Emma likes to recite a common family mantra when we go on walks together: "God loves all His Creatures, even bugs." Through her love of nature, I have made my own profound connection with it and look forward to our outdoor moving meditations.

- Emma always takes time to show love and appreciation to the special people in her world. Despite the fact that she sees her friends and teachers at school every day, she regularly gives them big hugs. She is generous with her affection, and it reminds me to do the same.

- Emma likes to share. She derives pleasure from sharing something of hers with another, from toys to books to snacks. I have learned that one of the most rewarding experiences is to share our gifts with others. It feels fantastic and supports the idea that we live in an unlimited, abundant world.

When I take the time to open my eyes and my heart to the magic, guidance, and wisdom of our little one, my life becomes much richer and more fulfilling. It's time I stop worrying so much about crossing items off my To-Do list and start learning the really important lessons from my phenomenal child.

CAREER

"Don't limit yourself. Many people limit themselves
to what they think they can do. You can go as far as
your mind lets you. What you believe,
remember, you can achieve."

—Mary Kay Ash

It Isn't About
the Pink Stuff

I AM A MARY KAY KID. My mother started her direct sales career with Mary Kay Cosmetics when I was six years old and remained a member of that awesome company until the day she died more than thirty years later. Whenever I mention the fact that my mom was in Mary Kay, the first question inevitably asked of me is, "Did she have a pink Cadillac?" Yep, she sure did. That freakin' pink car of hers, which was replaced every two years with a brand new model, was the bane of my existence growing up. It was a beautiful machine and certainly had all of the luxurious bells and whistles that one could ever want in an automobile. But I could never get over it's color; I was just so embarrassed by it's ... pinkness.

Mom got into Mary Kay in the early '70s, very soon after she and my dad divorced. Mary Kay was the perfect career option for my mother as she had used the product line for years, needed to earn more income than her nursing job provided, and wanted to be available when her children needed her. With Mom's natural affinity for the products and her remarkable gift of gab, she had all the makings of a successful Mary Kay businesswoman.

Before Mom started winning cars, furs, and diamonds, I would often tag along with her to the in-home sales presentations she made. By the time I was in third grade I could easily recite the five basic steps in the Mary Kay skin care line including their features, benefits, and proper application techniques. I was fluent in the company's extensive glamour line and could describe the key elements of conducting a recruiting interview. Through Mom's extraordinary efforts she quickly moved into a management role after building a large, highly productive team of salespeople. I was fortunate enough to travel around the country with her as she gave motivational speeches and taught sales training classes in front of huge groups of adoring females. I swear I met more women by the time I was ten years old than most people meet in a lifetime.

While Mom shared with me many details of her growing business, she did her best to shield me from the unpleasantries and disappointments. For example, I had no clue about the gravity of her weekly sales summary report. To me this report was just another Mary Kay form, similar to the order forms, skin care profiles, and consultant agreements that were stacked on her desk. What I didn't realize at the time is that the numbers Mom put in the little boxes on the sales report dictated what we were going to spend at the grocery store that week, if I was going to get a new pair of shoes for school, and how generous Santa was going to be that year.

A few months before Mom died I asked her to tell me about the most difficult aspects of her career. Mom immediately launched into a great story about her early Mary Kay days. She said, "Teeter, there was nothing harder than maintaining a positive attitude after being totally exhausted from a full day's work, having to drive my beat-up Datsun B-210 in a Minnesota snowstorm, hauling heavy pink product cases into some stranger's house, spending two hours on my aching feet in high heels, and selling one mascara. Trust me, honey, *that* was hard to do."

When I was growing up I never saw this emotionally taxing part of her business. Instead, Mom only exposed me to the positive side. She was, after all, the Queen of Positive Mental Attitude. Our two-bedroom apartment had stacks of inspirational books in every room, affirmations written on scraps of paper taped around the house, and mirrors next to each telephone so Mom could check her smile while speaking to a customer or recruit. Books and tapes from motivational gurus like Zig Ziglar, Tony Robbins, and Napoleon Hill were permanent fixtures in our home. My mom had a vision board before vision boards were cool.

No matter how many setbacks she endured, the woman never lost sight of the dream to run her own business. Through years of hard work and practicing the Law of Attraction, as well as her unwavering belief in herself and Spirit, Mom created the career she desired. She was able to provide for her family, earn a sizable income, have a beautiful home, take nice vacations, and most importantly, have the flexibility to do what she wanted, when she wanted. My mother never missed any of my piano recitals, school plays, choral performances, or other events that are so important to kids. Every day Mom was at home when I left for school and every day she was there when I returned. Quite simply, the company with the pink jars and the pink cars enabled my mother to *be there* for me.

Mary Kay had such a positive impact on my life that, while in my twenties, I thought I would try to make a go at it myself. I failed dismally at it—twice. Having to work when I didn't want to, talking to strangers, and booking classes were my downfalls. I could easily envision myself at the enviable national management level, not only from an income perspective but also from a responsibilities standpoint. The problem wasn't visualizing the future; it was doing the actual work in the present. I just couldn't or wouldn't get my butt out of the house to generate the sale. A viable direct sales business isn't made while sitting in one's cushy home office ordering product and making brochures. Eventually I had to surrender the fantasy of being my own boss (in Mary Kay at least), and continued down the corporate path until many interesting twists and turns brought me to my current vocation as a writer.

As I reflect on the tremendous influence that organization had on me, both as an MK kid and a struggling consultant, I feel badly I gave my mom so much grief about the pink car. I recently recalled a memory from long ago. After listening to her self-absorbed teen-age daughter blather on about the cheesiness of the family roadster, Mom calmly replied, "Teeter, it isn't about the pink stuff. It's about what the pink stuff provides us." Her observation was simple yet profound. Not only does it apply to those women who sell cosmetics but also to all who have chosen scrapbooks, candles, jewelry, plastic storage, or anything else found in a catalog as a means to provide for themselves and their families.

With age comes wisdom. Maturity has given me a deeper appreciation for all that goes into these entrepreneurial careers, and I honor each and every woman who decides to take it on. I now realize it's not about the pink stuff; it's about the green. These brave warrior women deserve my utmost respect regardless of the color of their cars. Bravo, ladies, for a job well done.

I Am Not My Title

❧

I AM A JILL OF ALL TRADES. In the twenty-five years I've been in the workforce I've been everything from a cashier to an executive. The title associated with my employment used to be important to me. Really important. For years I kept working in dreadful jobs because of the allure of The Next Big Title.

My first job was at McDonald's. At fourteen years of age I would walk to work several afternoons a week outfitted in my heinous polyester uniform and grease-stained visor. As a cashier I worked my tail off ringing-up orders, making fries, filling orders, and handling money. It was widely known among the Mickey D's staff that working the drive-thru was the most 'kick-ass' of all assignments. The drive-thru station was in its own little room, conveniently located far away from the din of the dining room. The lucky worker wore a hip-at-the-time headset, avoided mopping floors, cleaning tables and emptying garbage, and delivered the completed orders that other staffers toiled to assemble. That sounded like a pretty good deal to me, so I set my sights on becoming the next Drive-thru Girl.

Through serious hard work and a noteworthy amount of management butt-kissing, I quickly earned the coveted role. While it didn't have a formal title per se, all of my burger buddies openly acknowledged that this job was far superior to all others. Thus I had my first taste of ego gratification in the workplace.

Throughout my late teens and early twenties, I held a variety of jobs including swimming pool attendant, data entry clerk, office temp, and secretary. I would yearn for the day when I could walk into the big office with a window, sit in an overstuffed leather chair, talk on speakerphone, and delegate tasks to my loyal subordinates. The job of my fantasies always had super-cool titles: Advertising Coordinator, Manager of International Affairs, Director of Procurement, and Vice President of Marketing and Development. I didn't really know or care what the titles meant. I only knew that I wanted to be one of those fortunate souls some day. From my naïve vantage point, those positions sounded important and the people who held them must have been respected and appreciated.

In my mid-twenties, I parlayed a long-term temp job into a full-time secretary/office manager position for a growing company. Yay! The word 'manager' was in my title! Over the next few years I worked like a dog, often staying late and coming in on the weekends. I accepted any and all projects without complaint, eventually getting recognized by upper management and earning ever more prestigious job titles.

Over the next several years I climbed the rungs of the corporate ladder, rising from Manager to Senior Manager to Vice President. During my final months in the business world I finally landed in the high-rise office with a window and the big chair. How ironic it was to finally earn all of the trappings I desired only to discover I was miserable. Despite my success, I despised going to work everyday and my body was reacting to the stress. By the time I hit thirty I had developed ulcers and grinded my teeth, my complexion resembled the pizza I consumed on a regular basis, and my hair was falling out. Lovely.

After Spirit literally heaved me out of the corporate nest via two brutal layoffs (Thank you! Thank you! Thank you!), I dove into the alternative healing world as a licensed massage therapist and owner of a healing center. My funky new world provided a whole new set of titles with which to wrap myself around: Bodyworker, Reiki Master, Intuitive Healer, Meditation Guide, Yoga Instructor, and Workshop Facilitator to name a few. Woo hoo! Even though my new life didn't include being the Vice President of the Whatcheehoo Department, I still got off on possessing rather unique, glamorous, and mysterious job titles. It was always a thrill to meet someone new and tell him or her I was a Reiki Master by trade. It was like going back in time to junior high school and being one of the first girls in seventh grade to have a pair of authentic Jordache jeans. Inevitably my new acquaintance would don a curious and surprised look with just a hint of envy. Ahhh...the perfect combination to stroke my fragile ego.

But after my mom got sick, things that used to be important weren't anymore. Witnessing her conscious dying changed me forever, and a major chunk of my ego died when she did. Seeing her release her earthly attachments one by one gave me the inspiration to release some of my own. After she transitioned, my work priorities changed dramatically. I lost interest in my job title, where I worked, how much money I made, or frankly, what anyone thought about my choices. My incredible experience with Mom taught me how precious and brief life really is. I no longer wanted to kill myself at a job that wasn't absolutely in harmony with my desire or Divine Purpose. This realization of what is truly important led me to chuck it all and start from scratch. This time I would define myself from the inside out.

Today I am blessed to be able to live my passions, and my simple, unadorned job titles reflect them. I am an Author, Healer, and Speaker because I love to write, help people, and talk (just ask my beleaguered husband). Those activities make me happy; running a business or being a corporate climber does not. I've largely, but not entirely, let go of the need for the external world to validate me, and with that have given up a life of the fancy corner office. I'll never again be Theresa A. Rose, Senior Vice President of the

Department That Is Truly Important. But that's fine with me. Now I'm just Theresa, trying to feel as much joy as possible. Maybe that should be on my next and final business card: Theresa Rose, *Joy Seeker*.

From the Boardroom to the Treatment Room

I VAGUELY REMEMBER what it was like to put on panty hose, a business suit and high heels every day. My professional work history includes stints as a consultant, a senior manager of marketing and product development for a global telecommunications company and a vice president for a consulting firm. I spent many years as a frequent flier, traveling for project meetings, conferences, and client presentations. I knew people at the Delta Airlines counter better than I knew my own neighbors.

Five years ago I made the dramatic shift from a hard-as-nails road warrior to a soft-and-cuddly alternative healer. My last job as a holistic practitioner and healing center owner afforded me the opportunity to give away my high heels and spend the majority of my days barefoot listening to New Age music while performing energy healing treatments and leading meditation circles. It was quite a contrast from the hats I had worn before.

People ask me how I made such a dramatic shift in careers. As with everything in life, Spirit has a way of creating exactly what you need when you need it. I was laid off twice within ten months and couldn't find a job even after searching exhaustively. I researched, networked, applied, and interviewed until I was blue in the face but kept coming up empty. I was *not* the kind of woman who couldn't find a job; I had the right credentials, experience, interviewing skills, references, and most importantly, an insane desire to please. If I had difficulty finding a job, then there had to be something I was missing. It was then I started to realize that maybe, just maybe, I should start to employ one of the tired management clichés I was prone to using in team meetings: I needed to 'think outside the box'.

I found a new life outside the box in Sedona, Arizona. Due to my recent unemployment woes, Michael thought we needed to take a little vacation to "ground and re-center ourselves"; in other words, "to stop my wife's incessant whining". While in Sedona I went to a psychic reader just for shits and giggles, thinking I would take the hour to grill her on where I would find my next job. Assuming she was any good at predicting the future, I expected her to point me in the direction of either on-the-road consulting or real estate sales. These were shaping up to be the only possible employment options awaiting me at home. Neither one was particularly appealing but seemed to be my only choices short of being a fry-cook at Denny's.

Contrary to my expectations, the psychic told me I wasn't going to find another job in the business world; instead she told me that I was a healer. A healer?! What the hell did that mean? Needless to say, I was annoyed with this woman for wasting my time and money. Much of me wanted to write her intuitive reading off as goofy nonsense, yet I couldn't help but notice much of what she said had struck a chord in me. The next day I decided to get a second reading from another intuitive to see if I could get her to tell me what I wanted to hear.

Long story short, I went to three other intuitives that week, all of whom told me the exact same thing—that I was destined to be a healer and would no longer have a traditional business career. I initially wanted to disregard their advice as silly ramblings of spaced-out hippies. However, there was just one little problem. These messengers weren't crazy nutjobs from some 1-800 psychic hotline. They looked and acted like me. All were well-groomed, intelligent people who clearly articulated their positions using compelling logic and common sense. In short, they were 'normal'.

I asked one of them how she knew what she knew. She explained that in her mind's eye she saw a vision of me as a toy soldier forever marching forward. There appeared a wall in front of me that had never been there before (no job, no prospects, no success); I didn't know how to respond to the obstacle other than to blindly march forward. She suggested that the Universe placed the wall in front of me so I would be forced to move in a new direction. By turning my career in a new direction toward the healing profession as opposed to the business world, I could once again march forward freely without obstruction.

My hyper-analytical mind kicked into overdrive. What exactly did a healer do? How does one become a healer? Are there certifications? Is there a correspondence course I could take or an instructional book I could buy? One of the intuitives suggested I start down my healer's path by attending massage therapy school. She asked me, "Do you like massage?" Huh? I wondered if it was a trick question. I replied, "Are you kidding me? Of course I like massage! I get one as often as I can. Michael and I even own a massage table!" She reminded me how 'coincidental' it was that I already owned the major piece of equipment that healers use to conduct their sessions. Unbeknownst to me, my subconscious mind was already moving in the new direction.

All of the advice I received that week sounded crazy from my myopic viewpoint. I thought reading energy, receiving spiritual guidance, and trusting in a Higher Power was a bunch of cosmic muffiny, woo-woo stuff. Despite my left-brained protestations, everything these people told me that week felt right. With nothing else to lose, I started to entertain this kooky non-traditional path.

I saw two options available to me: 1) continue to look for some bullshit business job that I didn't really want, fail miserably, and then wallow in self-pity, or 2) give and receive massages each day as the local massage school web site had advertised. Hmmm...let's see...tough choice. Call me crazy, but I chose the latter. So began my transformation from corporate chick to intuitive healer.

From the very first day of class, I got hooked on therapeutic body-work, energy healing and the power of touch. Something inside me felt like I had come home. I was also blessed to have a classmate who was a Reiki Master. She taught me about Reiki, a powerful form of Japanese hands-on energy healing that would end up being a major influence in my life. Just a few months after graduation, I opened my own healing center and lovingly nurtured that business for over three years until shutting its doors after Mom died.

As I look back on my history in the business world, I can recall a lot of the negative aspects. I remember having to lay people off for no reason other than increasing profit margins, sitting in pointless meetings talking about what will happen at the next meeting, and wasting time creating useless Powerpoint presentations and Excel spreadsheets. I remember sprinting through the Atlanta airport with my laptop bag banging against my leg trying in vain to catch the last flight home. I remember driving from the Tampa International Airport at 2:30 in the morning, crossing over the Skyway Bridge in a raging tropical storm, and questioning, "This can't be what life is all about."

Even with all of the downsides of my business career, I wouldn't trade those experiences for the world. I earned my college degree while working full-time, met some fascinating people, and gained a considerable amount of knowledge and skill that I use to this day.

On the other end of the vocational spectrum, I loved being a hippy-dippy healer as well. I treasured the warm hugs I received from attendees of my classes and guided meditations, the loving relationships I developed with staff, clients, and students, and the many instances of helping people empower themselves through bodywork, meditation, movement and conscious choice. But most importantly, I treasured being home with my husband and daughter every night instead of being holed-up in a Marriott Courtyard hotel room in Colorado Springs preparing for the next morning's project status meeting. Plus there was one final bonus: I *never* had to wear those God-awful control-top panty hose again.

BEAUTY
OR THE BEAST

I WOULD BE WILLING TO BET that most men don't get promoted based on the size of their penis or pecs (the sole exception being the porn industry). However, a woman's appearance and demeanor often play a major role in the organizational doors that get opened for her. I have spent several years in the corporate Thunderdome and have observed, and many of my gal pals will corroborate, that women who are actively pursuing career advancement in male-dominated companies are often characterized in one of two ways: Beauty or the Beast.

My work experience showed me that there are two types of women that tend to rise to upper echelons of management in big business—the *Melrose Place*-like slut or the raging bitch. Naturally, both archetypes had to have tiny waistlines, because most members of the executive boys club simply won't abide fat chicks regardless of how competent they are. At top levels of management, men can be old, bald, and have a beer gut that has its own zip code, but their female counterparts are expected to look like Melanie Griffith in *Working Girl*. Of course these women are not actually bitches or whores, but those characteristics are often what they had to highlight in order to get recognized, much less respected, among the musk of masculinity.

This isn't to say that one archetype is ultimately more likely to succeed than the other. The Beauty's dazzling smile may initially generate more lucrative opportunities, but the Beast's verbal whip may earn her more responsibility, not to mention generate higher levels of output squeezed from her terrified minions. The truly successful women in these companies can capture both elements equally. They can bat their pretty eyes to their adoring male associates while destroying anyone foolish enough to cross them. I myself was given the nickname of 'The Velvet Hammer' when I was enmeshed in the cutthroat business world.

The other day I went to lunch with a friend of mine, a stunning woman who works for a premier interior design firm. We dished the dirt on how unfair it was that professional women desiring upward mobility were expected to remain thin, beautiful, impeccably dressed and fabulously quaffed at all times. My friend told me a story about the feminine conundrum from the Beauty's perspective. A few weeks into her job a senior executive not-so-subtly mentioned that "a woman like her" should make every effort to ensure she doesn't come across as ditzy or stupid in front of clients and vendors. Since this guy hadn't taken the time to ascertain her credentials or skills, he was clearly basing his opinion on her looks. His ridiculous presumption caused my friend no end of aggravation. She now works like a Tibetan Sherpa scaling the south face of Everest in order to prove her competence, simply because she is disgustingly gorgeous.

For those women that are able to pull off the size 2 Chanel suit with a whip and a smile, they are still most likely paddling upstream because of their inherent disaffection for the nectar of the boardroom barbarians: playing golf and watching ESPN. The sad truth is that there are 40-watt dudes all over this fair land experiencing greater financial and professional rewards than their more competent female coworkers simply because they have killer golf handicaps and are human highlight reels of last weekend's games. (Many women quizzically view this obsession with hitting a tiny white ball and watching TV shows of other guys and their balls as the ultimate time-sucker.) Every Sunday these men sit in their La-Z-Boys watching sports for hours while their wives are taking care of the kids, doing laundry, grocery shopping, cleaning, and tackling a mountain of other necessary tasks. Life just ain't fair sometimes, sisters.

There are, however, silver linings in the dark chauvinistic clouds of the workplace. I'd like to praise the rare gems among the management ranks, those conscious managers who don't fall into the knuckle-dragger or doofus categories. These enlightened souls look beyond the surface. They hire smart people who work hard, get treated well, earn a nice living, and eventually get promoted, regardless of their genitalia.

If you don't work for one of these fabulous organizations, things may not be so rosy. You may find yourself banging your head against the glass ceiling at work because you are too hot, not hot enough, too mean, not mean enough, or just too female. If this feels true for you, maybe it's time to reevaluate your situation. Women from all industries and walks of life are starting to see the professional injustices around them and shout, "No more!" They are seeking better jobs with conscious companies, starting their own businesses, or completely reinventing themselves with exciting and enjoyable new careers in which upward mobility is not driven by their cup size. Whether they are striking-out on their own or actively seeking better employment with another company, the result is the same: women are starting to reject the old-school machismo paradigm. Cue the Helen Reddy sing-a-long!

If you want a better job than you currently have, *create it*. Place your order with Spirit in your regular meditations and prayers. Start talking it up with your friends and attend functions with other smart, savvy people. Visualize yourself having the career of your dreams. If you continually focus your energy on manifesting the perfect new career where you get paid for what you are worth, the Universe will eventually respond by placing that opportunity in front of you. Imagine being powerful yet feminine, getting recognized for your efforts, cashing big, fat paychecks, all the while refusing to sell out to the boys upstairs! That, my friend, is my definition of a sizzlin' hot babe.

No Time Off
for Good Behavior

I T IS PATENTLY UNFAIR how most companies reward their highly-productive employees. They assign them *more work*. What's up with that? It should be just the opposite. If you get your work done in a shorter timeframe than the other guy, then you should be able to do what our children do: get out a coloring book and have fun until the slower kids catch up. Instead we get another pile of crap hoisted upon us while the slacker in the next cubicle takes twice as long to finish half the work. I am offended by this blatant contradiction of a fundamental law of the Universe. One should be rewarded, not punished, for a job well done.

When I was a hired-gun technology consultant in the Washington, DC area years ago, my peers and I were strongly encouraged to work ungodly hours for our clients, all of which were billed out the ass. Of course my salary didn't change if I worked forty hours a week or seventy, but I got the distinction of being at the top of the Revenue Earned and Hours Worked monthly reports in my firm. Yippee skippy. That and five bucks would buy me a decaf mocha at Starbucks.

This glaring inequity was the primary reason I decided to venture out on my own as an independent consultant. I couldn't abide working sixty to seventy-five hours every week and cashing the same paycheck amount as the goofball putting in thirty-five hours on a good week. Once I became an independent contractor, my paychecks reflected my actual hours worked. I'll admit that it certainly felt good to be handsomely paid every two weeks. The greatest benefit of striking out on my own was not the big dollars; it was knowing that I was getting properly compensated for my efforts. If I chose to work crazy hours, then at least I'd get paid for it.

The gravy train came to a screeching halt when my primary client informed me that I needed to convert to full-time employee status or lose the gig entirely. Being faced with the prospect of having to pound the pavement for other consulting jobs wasn't very appealing so I decided to leave the independent consulting world behind. Even though I was promoted to senior management, my take-home pay was cut by more than half. Since Michael and I were DINKs at the time—Double Income, No Kids—my decrease in salary wasn't a tragedy of epic proportions. But what was a tragedy was my boss's expectation that I continue my insane work schedule while earning less than half the money. Naturally, being the chronic overachiever that I am, I did exactly that.

I take a lot of pride in my work and will put in as many hours as it takes to not only get a job done, but to get it done exceedingly well. I wish I could say that my hearty Midwestern stock was the sole cause of my fanatical work ethic; the truth is a little darker. I worked late, came in on weekends and had sleepless nights because I yearned for Daddy's, er, my boss's approval. I wanted him to recognize me, gush over me, reward me, and above all, appreciate me. (This desperate need for male acceptance resulted in having multiple embarrassing, full-blown crushes.) I can't even tell you how friggin' hard I worked to earn the Employee of the Month award in the mid-90s. The damn thing wasn't even one of those acrylic statuettes! It was a cheesy certificate printed on the office

LaserJet minutes before our monthly staff meeting. Yet it was one of my most coveted possessions.

I know I am not alone in the world of occupational bloodletting. There are thousands of employees just like me who work like indentured servants not only for the steady paycheck, but more importantly, for the recognition and approval of their employers. Admittedly some of them are going well above and beyond the call of duty in pursuit of the illusion of job security. However, I would argue that the majority of them are busting their butts because they simply love the feeling of being loved. They'll do whatever it takes to earn the warm fuzzies of an appreciative boss/parent figure regardless of how fleeting they may be. What is our reward for all of this hard work? More hard work! We keep running full-speed on the hamster wheel until our bosses decide they don't need us anymore, our families don't remember us anymore, or our bodies don't work anymore.

Although I no longer work for someone else, I still find myself pushing harder than I need to, giving myself unrealistic deadlines, and critically judging my productivity against impossible ideals. My work obsession is an ancient habit and an unfortunate by-product of unprocessed gunk from old emotional wounds. As part of the healing process, I'm trying to address my performance mania so I can actually enjoy my career. There's a novel concept! Having grown weary of taking on more work than I can ever reasonably handle, I want to take my foot off the gas pedal. After twenty-five years in the workforce, I'm finally ready to have some fun! I think I'll break open a brand new box of 64-count crayons and start coloring for a while.

FAILING FORWARD

❧

FAILURE IS SOMETHING at which I have become quite adept. In fact, much of my professional life could be characterized as a series of employment misadventures. One job after the other was a flop of some kind, each one bringing with it a brand new chance to berate myself.

I failed as a Mary Kay consultant because I didn't do the necessary tasks as often as required. Moreover, my subterranean self-esteem had me frequently second-guessing my persuasive abilities. (Why would any woman in her right mind take beauty advice from someone like me?) This failure was particularly hard to accept because of my mom's phenomenal track record. While she never said anything to me about my poor performance, I knew she was disappointed when I threw in the pink towel. She wanted the dream of the mother-daughter dynamic duo as much as I did.

I also failed at two of my senior management jobs. I was a casualty of "reductions in force", a sanitized way of describing mass layoffs. Of course one could argue that layoffs aren't the same thing as being fired. From my unsteady perch, however, not going to work or getting paid any longer felt an awful lot like getting fired. Those of us who were laid off understood that our jobs were disposable and so were we.

The most recent (and most public) failure was my stint as the owner of a healing center. After graduating from massage school I embarked on what I thought would be my career zenith: opening EnergyWorks, a gathering place for the healing arts. Stung from the spate of recent firings, er, layoffs, I craved a soft, cozy, and safe womb of my own creation. Since its inception, I vowed to keep the focus of EnergyWorks on promoting healing, community, and connection to the Divine. I intended that the cold, harsh, analytical elements of business were going to be a thing of the past.

I never looked at EnergyWorks as a business venture, instead seeing it more as a second child. My occupational bundle of love received much of my energy from the moment of her birth. I gave her everything a new baby business could want: the perfect location, a fabulous name, an elegant marketing campaign, beautiful furnishings, exceptional staff, and outstanding services, classes and events. I nurtured her nearly every day and most evenings. I ate, slept, and breathed EnergyWorks for three solid years.

Alas, all my hard work and prayers paid off! Through my efforts and those of my amazing team of professionals, we succeeded in creating 'the gathering place for the healing arts' that I had envisioned. My staff and I treated hundreds of clients, helping them to live more healthfully and powerfully. We hosted weekly events where members of the community gathered for yoga and meditation. I also taught scores of students the ancient practice of Reiki energy healing, connecting them to the Divine source of healing power inherent in all of us. What I had vowed to accomplish for EnergyWorks I had done with flying colors. The only problem was that it wasn't making any money.

For those three years the center was open, I didn't look at one crucial factor one must pay attention to when running a business: the numbers. I had no earthly idea how much income we were making or what expenses we were incurring. All I knew was that more often than not I had to ask Michael for a check from our personal finances to cover costs at the end of the month. I was deathly afraid to look too closely at the numbers for fear that it would force me to make unpleasant decisions that would affect what truly mattered to me.

To be sure, if making money was the most important factor I could have been far more prudent; I certainly was when I worked for other companies. I could have paid my staff less money, hiring mediocre practitioners and sacrificing the quality of our services. I could have charged higher fees, minimizing customer loyalty and reducing referrals. I could have skimped on the beauty of the facility itself, making it look and feel like every other humdrum medical office. Since I didn't want any of those consequences, I chose to immerse myself in the healing part of the healing center while ignoring the owning part.

When my mother died, my priorities changed dramatically. After taking several weeks off to wrap up Mom's affairs and honor my bereavement, I returned to the once-cozy confines of my beloved healing center. I was surprised to discover that I simply didn't enjoy owning EnergyWorks anymore. Managing the business became a lifeless, depressing exercise, made even worse by the absence of my mother greeting me from the receptionist desk every day. In response to my growing malaise, I found solace in writing. My literary confessions quickly became my greatest source of healing and most joyful creative outlet.

Life was more precious now, and I no longer wanted to spend half my waking hours at a job I didn't like. Consequently, when the center's lease ended I elected not to renew it, bidding a tearful *adieu* to the business to which I had given so much of myself. While this was a difficult decision that disappointed many people, it felt absolutely right to me as it freed up my time and energy to focus exclusively on my true passions of writing and facilitating.

For years I perceived my Mary Kay flame-outs, the corporate layoffs, and my healing center debacle as monumental career disasters. I was embarrassed by their outcomes and my personal culpability in them. As a child I grew up believing that the only acceptable grade was an A, with all other grades causing justifiable judgment and disappointment. As an adult my occupational report card seemed to contain far too many D-minuses; not as catastrophic as receiving an F, but pretty friggin' close.

Thankfully I now see things differently. I understand those employment stints were not failures but portals that led me to something better. Mary Kay brought me to several interesting positions in the business world, which in turn brought many formative experiences and a fateful introduction to one Michael Rose. My corporate jobs brought me to massage school, which in turn helped me to become a spiritual healer and teacher. EnergyWorks brought me to my current vocation as writer and speaker, a career I find deeply fulfilling. Each of these opportunities was perfectly orchestrated and executed, almost as if they were Divinely guided. Hmmm...coincidence? I think not.

Failure is an illusion. Everything that happens to us contains a precious gift, either in the form of a valuable life lesson or the presentation of an exciting new door through which to walk. This is especially true when we fall face-first into the mud. By finally accepting this fact, I have opened up to new levels of happiness and success while no longer being consumed with self-recrimination or fear of failure. I now trust that Spirit is watching out for me, supporting me, and providing me exactly what I need, even if I don't understand it at the time.

I like to think I have the Universe's Most Powerful Career Counselor workin' for me. My Divine Counselor has helped my writing immeasurably by supplying me with inspiration and the perfect words in which to express it. My vocation is nearly as fun as a vacation, and it is in delightful harmony with the rest of my life. Thankfully, my spiritual practice has made me increasingly aware of the signs pointing me toward the Next Big Opportunities whenever they present themselves and readies me to gracefully accept them. After twenty-five painful years of crawling, scratching, climbing, and falling off the career ladder, I have finally reached the pinnacle of true success: the realization that no matter what I do, I'll never be a failure. Whether I am basking in my accomplishments or blushing from my embarrassments, I know that everything happens exactly as it should. What a relief.

DEATH

"I still miss those I loved who are no longer with me
but I find I am grateful for having loved them.
The gratitude has finally conquered the loss."

—RITA MAE BROWN

THE CONVERSATION
ON THE COUCH

I T'S A STRANGE, SURREAL THING to sit one's own mother down and tell her she's going to die—soon. That is what happened to me on June 19th, 2006. Mom was a lifelong smoker, ate junk food every day, had a fair amount of unprocessed grief, and seemed to have an acute allergic reaction to exercise. Based on my experience as a healing practitioner I knew her tiny body could withstand that kind of abuse for only so long.

My worst fears were confirmed during a trip I took with Mom a few days before that conversation in June. Mom, Jean and I were going to a spa in Miami for a few days. For over two years, my mother had been working as a receptionist at EnergyWorks, my healing center, without receiving a single paycheck. Treating her to a getaway at a world-class spa seemed to be the perfect thank-you for the generous love and support she provided. During the first night of our vacation I realized that Mom was really sick. She had camouflaged it so well during the daytime hours, and I told myself previously that her occasional coughs were normal. However, these late-night hacking episodes were so violent that many times over the course of the evening I wondered if she would make it until morning.

I spent the next two days fretting about what I knew intuitively to be true—Mom was dying. During the last night of our stay Mom had a coughing fit that simply had no end. I listened to her struggle for breath for what seemed an eternity and finally couldn't stand it any longer. Crawling into bed with her, I placed my hands on her back as she lied on her side and sent her as much healing energy as I could. Within seconds, I felt the unforgettable cold-steel sensation of treating someone with cancer. My hands were like heavy-duty magnets attached to her as her body instinctively pulled massive amounts of energy through me in order to quell the pain. After a few minutes the coughing stopped completely, and I spent the rest of the night in that same position, willing myself to heal her with my touch.

On the last morning of our trip, my friend and I went for a walk near the hotel. It was then that I confided my worst fears to her. Jean, a very sensitive and highly-intuitive soul, did the best thing she could have ever done—she agreed with me. Rather than trying to convince me that I was reading too much into Mom's cough or spinning it in a positive, hopeful light, she gave me what I most needed: the truth. She helped me embrace reality rather than enabling me down the path of denial. Her witnessing of my mom's illness allowed me to share my fears and ultimately have the courage to name them. I decided to name them to Mom herself a few days later.

The night we returned home, I wept at the thought of what I was about to do. I kept thinking, "What if I'm wrong? What if she isn't dying? How much will my words hurt her? Will telling her permanently damage our relationship?" Michael responded to my second-guessing by simply asking, "Do you think you're wrong?" Every time I asked it of myself, the answer kept coming back a resounding *no*. In my heart I knew that Mom was dreading having to tell her children of her condition, and I wanted to free her from that burden.

I will never forget my conversation on Mom's couch that Monday afternoon in June. She had come home early from EnergyWorks ostensibly to eat lunch, although I knew she did so because she was exhausted from trying to keep up appearances. Before I walked in the door, I steadied my nerves with some deep breathing exercises, and grounded my energy into the Earth as I had taught my students and clients to do hundreds of times before. I was armed with my tiny sheet of paper on which I had written several talking points. I knew if I didn't have it with me I would either forget one of the points or chicken-out altogether. The list included:

- I know you're sick
- It's OK, I won't ask you to quit smoking
- You don't have to see a doctor if you don't want to
- You can stop working at EnergyWorks
- You should go anywhere and do anything you want
- We need to call Al and Doug (my brothers) ASAP
- We need to get legal arrangements in place
- No more sleepovers with Emma

As I proceeded down the list a wave of calm and relief washed over her. She said she knew she was very ill and was grateful I had addressed it. Then I brought up the last item—I told Mom I no longer felt it was safe for Emma to stay overnight with her. Gingerly, I explained it wouldn't be fair to Emma if something happened to her and my little girl was left alone and afraid, having to deal with God-knows-what. I had never before seen such a look of anguish on my mother's face; even thinking about that moment now makes my guts churn. I *hated* having to take away one of the best things in my mother's life, but I needed to look out for the well-being of my young, impressionable daughter. In the end, Mom reluctantly agreed but was heartsick nonetheless.

Within two weeks of that initial conversation, Mom saw a specialist and had a medical procedure to confirm that she did, in fact, have inoperable lung cancer. The doctor gave her a prognosis of six to eighteen months to live, and the tumor was likely not going to be materially affected by radiation or chemotherapy treatment. Given her prognosis, Mom decided to begin hospice immediately. I honored her decision and tried to support her in whatever way she needed. My oldest brother Allan moved in with Mom right after learning of her illness, providing her with an enormous amount of happiness and comfort in the final months.

I vividly remember a private conversation Mom and I had a day or so after the prognosis consultation with her doctor. She said, "Teeter, I'd like you to tell me what you think as far as timing." My mother knew I had intuitive abilities and could read the body's energy pretty well. I prayed this question would never come up, as I had already asked it of myself a hundred times since the spa drama. Claiming I was just some "chick with an opinion", I told her I didn't want to answer it. She pressed me for the information and said she really wanted to know. I breathed deeply, closed my eyes, and said, "around Thanksgiving, Ma." This was really difficult for me to say because it was only four-and-a-half months away. Mom nodded knowingly and said, "Honey, thank you for telling me. I know that was hard." Mom died four days after Thanksgiving.

As I look back on that significant time in my life, I am glad I had the courage to mention the elephant in the room. From the beginning I approached my mother's death honestly and without hesitation, and she grew to trust me explicitly because of it. Mom frequently confided her deepest feelings to me because she knew I would listen with compassion, stay present in her darkest moments, and *never* minimize her experience because it was too uncomfortable. There were many times of great heartache, but I wanted to consciously participate in my mother's death, with purpose and intention. Breaking from my well-worn pattern of dysfunction, I didn't hide from the eventuality by anesthetizing myself.

Several years before she died, I asked my mother what she wanted to do with the rest of her life. She was in a very unhappy place at the time and nothing seemed to bring her joy. I said to her, "There's got to be somewhere you want to go, something you want to see, someone you want to meet, or some food you want to eat. Is there *anything* you want to do that would make you really happy?" She pondered this question only briefly and responded, "Nope, I've done everything I've wanted to do." At that moment I knew her remaining time in this world would be brief. No one can live for very long without some reason to get up in the morning.

My mother died of lung cancer and I believe she chose it on some unconscious level. She repeatedly ignored the physical warning signs and chose a lifestyle, both physical and emotional, that was not conducive to longevity. I don't resent Mom for leaving us so quickly, nor do I resent the cigarettes that facilitated her demise. The choices she made were hers, not mine, and I don't have a right to judge them. Does it matter anyway how someone leaves this world? Would my experience of loss be fundamentally different if she would have died in an accident or from the effects of another disease? At the end of the day, she would have left us either way.

The biggest regret my mother had about dying was the fact that she wasn't going to be able to hold her grandchildren anymore. It was in those times of her greatest pain when I would share with her my fervent belief that she *will* see them from The Other Side and we would all be together again one day. I tried to keep this light of hope burning bright in her, not only for her sake, but also for my own and that of my daughter.

During the year after her death, I was blessed to have many special moments with Mom's spirit. I can honestly say without a shadow of a doubt that my mother is still here watching over us. My greatest gift back to my mother has been to teach Emma this new language of Spirit. My daughter and I experience loving interactions with Mom's spirit by simply centering ourselves, quieting our minds and opening our hearts. Blessedly, Mom's final and greatest wish was granted. She remains an ongoing part of the lives of her loved ones, now and always.

DEATH THROUGH THE
EYES OF A CHILD

MY DAUGHTER ADORED HER MIM. Mim was the nickname Emma had for her grandma, and they loved spending time with each other. While at Mim's house, Emma got to bake chocolate chip cookies, watch TV, put on fancy makeup, and wear her grandma's favorite high heels. During sleepovers, my child also got to eat ice cream in bed, stay up as late as she wanted, and enjoy many other privileges granted exclusively by grandparents. Even though Emma was only five years old at the time, the witnessing of her grandmother's passage into the Spirit World was just as emotional for her as it was for the rest of the family.

Right after Mom was diagnosed with cancer, Michael and I agreed to tell Emma about her grandmother's illness as soon as possible. We hadn't figured out exactly how to broach the sensitive subject, and to complicate matters, Emma's birthday was just days away. He and I decided to wait until after her birthday to tell her. As usual, Emma had her own idea of how things should go. A few days after our discussion, Michael and I found Emma curled-up on the floor of our living room. When we asked her what was wrong, she told us about Mim being sick and how she knew that Mim was going back to God. Emma was understandably upset, and my sudden tears made her sadness even greater. Even in the midst of this emotional upheaval, I was proud that my daughter intuitively picked up on Mim's illness before we had made it known to her.

Over the next several months, Emma and I had many conversations about where Mim would go after she died, and my little one would vividly describe Mim's next home as the Castle in the Sky. The Castle was a fascinating place where God welcomed everyone who passed away. It was filled with music, dancing, and lights, and as Emma said, "there are fireworks of love *every night!*" She loved to draw colorful pictures of the Castle and would joyfully include Mim, her grandma Andreé, her cousin Sammy, and several other angels. Emma was very proud of these drawings and gave them all to her grandma. Mom cherished these simple gifts and placed them by her bedside, taking great comfort from them whenever a wave of fear came over her.

As Emma watched her grandma physically deteriorate, she held fast to the belief that Spirit was taking good care of Mim. She once said she could see the angels that were waiting to take Mim to the Castle. Emma would discuss these things freely with her grandmother, and my mom found peace in knowing that her grandbaby was showing us all how to process her death openly and fearlessly.

A few days after Mom died, Emma asked me to describe for her exactly how the event happened. Later that evening I brought Emma into my mother's home and laid her down on the bed where her grandma took her last breath. I described every last detail about Mom's beautiful, peaceful and powerful transition including the presence of angels that Emma had previously mentioned. Without words, the two of us held each other and sobbed. Afterward Emma was glad to know that Mim had gone into the Light exactly as she had predicted and Mom had wanted.

Weeks later Michael and I took our daughter to see the movie *Charlotte's Web*. Near the end of the movie when Charlotte passes on, Emma sat on my lap and bawled her little green eyes out. The three of us held each other and cried throughout the rest of the movie. Even after the movie Emma cried in the car for another twenty minutes. Michael and I were grateful for the celluloid spider that helped our little one's grieving process, enabling her to deeply feel the emotions surrounding death. As we all continue to grieve for our loss, I welcome and embrace all future opportunities to hold my daughter tightly, cry with her, and remember how much we love and miss our wonderful Mim.

A Painful Reminder

CB

ONE OF THE THINGS my dying mother asked of me was to be her personal representative. As such, I was legally responsible for the administration of her estate. This was not an insignificant undertaking. Months before she died I began managing a host of legal and financial matters on her behalf. After she passed, I orchestrated the enormous task of removing every last item from her home. I distributed countless objects of clothing, jewelry, knick-knacks, furniture, dishes, and pictures to various recipients. In addition, I also coordinated three very special memorial celebrations held across the country. (Only a woman like my mother would have not one, but three.) When the last memorial was done and her house was empty, I thought I could take a breath and finally get past the sting of her death. I was wrong; I forgot about taxes.

In addition to combing through a year's worth of receipts to find both personal and business deductions for Michael and me, I also had to go through 'The Box'. The Box contained all of Mom's papers that I simply couldn't bring myself to go through immediately after her death. It included every last scrap of paper from her desk, nightstand, and bedside magazine rack. I purposely kept The Box hidden in our garage, willing it to evaporate so I wouldn't have to deal with its contents. Alas, all hopes for spontaneous combustion proved fruitless, and last week's call from the tax accountant forced me to open the damn thing.

Initially I was thunderstruck by the sheer volume of material to be processed. There were piles of letters, cards and photos, her colorful pads of paper containing her multiple to-do lists, and of course, bills and receipts. At first I spent lots of time solemnly reviewing each piece, crying when I saw her picture and laughing when I saw her doodles. Continuing at that pace would have had me going through papers well past April 15th if I didn't get my ass in gear. Consequently, I plowed through the exercise as quickly and impersonally as I could, trying to disassociate myself with it. I robotically entered data into the spreadsheet as if it had no meaning—Date: 7/07/06, Description: Lakewood Ranch Medical Center, Amount: $2,500. Yet memories and visions seeped past my protective wall and into my consciousness.

While reviewing Mom's credit card statements and checkbook, I discovered unknown tidbits about her final weeks. On October 21st she went to Marina Jack's for her final birthday celebration so she could see the water one more time. On November 11th my brother Allan took her to Ruby Tuesday's for her last venture out of the house. (I imagined her ordering her favorite entrée of chicken fingers and fries!) On November 20th she received her last massage treatment from Rob, and I specifically remembered it as being one of her happiest final days. Each piece of data excavated memories that I did my best to stifle. After several exhausting days, I finished the tax preparation material and mailed it to the CPA. What a relief it was to have the chore over and done with. Ha! Not quite.

Days later Mom's attorney and I were on the telephone discussing another estate matter. About an hour after the conversation, I encountered a minor technical issue with my computer. Nothing I tried was fixing the problem, and I was getting more pissed-off by the minute. Despite my attempts to calm down, I couldn't shake my growing anger. After a while, I was totally out of control, heatedly banging my fists on the desk and screaming at the computer as loud as I could. Physically quaking from my bubbling rage, I stormed out of the office. As I stood next to the kitchen counter, I looked around for something I could throw, smash, or rip—anything that would release this violent energy within me. I found a book on the countertop, grabbed it, and slammed it down as hard as I could. Unfortunately, my index fingernail also caught on the counter; the force of my outburst caused my entire nail to pull back from my finger. I doubled over, fell to the tile floor, and screamed from the intensity of the pain.

As I sat crumpled and sobbing on the floor, my tears of pain and anger changed to tears of sorrow and grief. I was no longer crying over my throbbing finger; I was crying over how much I missed Mom. Sitting there holding my wounded hand to my wounded heart, I let myself feel the loss of my mother to my very core. I wailed, "I'll never be able to give you a hug again! I'll never be able to see you make cookies with Emma again! I'll never hear you laugh again!" I continued to weep for all the moments that will never happen. Eventually my tears subsided, my anger melted away, and my sorrow diminished. My purge on the kitchen floor helped lighten the load I had carried on my heavy heart ever since The Box was pried open.

For many days afterward, the big purple bruise on my finger served as a reminder from Spirit. It reminded me to be present in the moment. It reminded me to express my feelings when they surface instead of bottling them up for future processing. Most importantly it reminded me to honor the emotional complexities of grief.

The agony of saying farewell to a loved one doesn't end after the funeral. Grief is not a simple emotion that can be easily packaged and put away when real life resumes. Days, weeks, months, or years later, tears of sorrow will be shed because of some memory that surfaces. My tears will not and should not be dampened, for they remind me of how much I loved my mother. Honoring those tears is helping me to heal and allows me to remember the place she will forever occupy in my heart. My latest reminder was a painful lesson to be sure, but one that I was grateful to have learned.

THE RIGHT WORDS
AT THE RIGHT TIME

MY FAMILY AND I will be making the trek up north to South Dakota for Memorial Day weekend. Given that my mother passed away in late November, we had to wait until the Spring thaw before the memorial bench could be put in place at the local cemetery. Over the last few months, I have been experiencing a lot of emotions about this trip, not the least of which is fear. How would I explain cremation, burial, and other sensitive, death-related topics to my five-year old?

Soon after Mom's death I openly shared many things about that mystical evening with Emma, but never did we discuss the more practical aspects of her passing. Frankly, I didn't know how to describe hospice workers picking up Mom's body or the nitty-gritties of cremation. Instead I chose to focus on Mom's voyage back to Spirit and how she is always with us in our hearts. Given my mother's frequent spiritual visitations, it hadn't been difficult to do. Yet our Memorial Day trip was looming ever nearer, and I needed to find the words soon.

While taking my daily walk with Jean, I mentioned my dread of bringing up the issue of cremation with my little one. I didn't want

Emma getting traumatized by the thought of her grandmother's body burning to ashes, nor did I want her to be confused when other family members view the memorial bench and say, "There's Grandma." Immediately after sharing my fears, I received a strong message from Spirit on what approach I would take. I would explain to Emma the ancient practice of a funeral pyre where people use the sacred power of fire to burn away the physical bodies of those who have moved on to the Spirit World. I would explain how natural it is to return Mim's body back to its source, our beloved Mother Earth. I would make sure she understood that it isn't Mim burning at all, but merely her body that she no longer needed. We would finish our talk by discussing where her grandma really is. Alas, Spirit supplied me with the perfect answer to my parenting dilemma.

Not at all surprisingly, the very next morning Emma walked into our bedroom holding the small pewter urn that contains some of my mother's ashes. This shiny metal heart had been resting in the same place in our meditation room for almost four months, and not once had Emma asked about it. Yet less than a day after I figured out how I was going to broach the subject, in walks Emma with the urn in her tiny hands. At that moment I felt an overwhelming sense of gratitude to Spirit for giving me the intuitive insight on how to address this delicate topic, and to my child for so sweetly opening the dialogue.

Over the next few hours Emma and I had an incredible experience. We talked about Mim and the difference between her physical self and who she is in spirit. We recalled lots of stories of how Mim had visited us since her death, often through dreams, animal encounters, and visions. I then took Emma to a local cemetery where I showed her the inurnments of other people who chose cremation, and we walked by the gravesites of those who chose burial. We had a wonderful time on our field trip! She told me she really felt God there and thought it was a pretty place that she'd like to visit again.

Thank goodness this latest emotional hurdle is behind me. I will now be able to fully participate in the upcoming memorial ceremony without worrying about my daughter's fear or confusion. Once again, thank you, Spirit, for providing me the perfect words when I need them most.

MUSIC TO CRY TO

❧

DON'T YOU SOMETIMES FEEL like retreating into the corner and bawling your eyes out? I sure do. Whenever I am in serious need of a crying jag, I reach for my trusty iPod where I have a playlist designated for those occasions. It's called *Music To Cry To* and includes an hour's worth of songs that bring me to tears each and every time I hear them. Why on Earth would I choose such a depressing pastime? Because there are moments when my pent-up emotions bubble beneath the surface, and neither avoidance nor any amount of blah-blah-blah will release them. Sometimes I just gotta cry 'em out.

This all came about a few months before Mom died when I was driving Emma to school one morning. I was exhausted as I was in the midst of caring for my rapidly deteriorating mother while trying to keep everything else in my life afloat. My fatigue made me edgy about every little thing, so I wasn't up for our typical Mom/Daughter banter. For some reason I clicked on the radio. This was peculiar as we usually spent our car rides either talking with each other or listening to CDs. After flipping through the dial a few times I landed on a station that was playing the popular country hit, "Live Like You Were Dying" by Tim McGraw. I was instantly transfixed.

156

The ballad describes a man with a terminal illness appreciating the time he has left with his loved ones. By the last refrain I was a complete puddle. Emma was worried about me as she hadn't yet seen her mother totally lose it. I parked the car and invited her to sit up in the front seat with me. We hugged each other tightly for several minutes, and I explained to her that what we just heard touched the place in my heart that was so sad that Mim was dying. Emma cried too, and in her sweet and earnest way suggested that maybe I shouldn't listen to that song anymore! I assured her that listening to it actually made me feel better as I was able to let out some of the unhappiness that had built-up over time. After our tearful heart-to-heart, we both felt much better.

This initial session of music therapy prompted me to create my very own playlist of grieving tunes. I included the Tim McGraw song as well as several of Mom's favorites. During her illness she repeatedly listened to a handful of tunes, finding comfort in the words and enjoying the music while praying for her peaceful return to Spirit. These songs were so important to her that my brothers and I chose to play them at each of the memorial services. Since then, anytime I hear "My Way", "One Moment in Time", "When I Get Where I'm Going" or "Long Time Sun", I have an immediate Pavlovian response: hear songs, weep like a baby. When I surrender and give in to the tears, I find myself connecting deeply to her spirit as she fills my heart once again.

Emma has joined in on the music therapy too, occasionally playing one of her grandmother's favorite Dean Evenson meditation CDs. Emma calls it her "sacred music" and gets very introspective upon hearing it. Listening to this album helps my daughter process her grief while enabling her to quiet her mind and connect to her grandma's energy.

As time passes, the intense sadness of my mother's death is easing up a bit. I can now recall stories about Mom with more joy and less melancholy. My family and I can even joke about some of her silly and embarrassing moments instead of being so precious about her memory. In that spirit, in addition to playing my *Music To Cry To* playlist every once in a while, I also find myself queuing-up Dean Martin's "Ain't That a Kick in the Head". After all, Mom was always a huge Dino fan.

THE HIGH HEEL
AND THE CARDINAL

MY MOTHER WAS FORTUNATE ENOUGH to put her affairs in order before she died. Of the many loose ends Mom was anxious to tie up, she was most concerned about how her personal belongings were to be distributed in order to prevent potential conflicts between family members. So one weekend she and I scoured every inch of her house as she identified each possession and who was to receive it. For hours we discussed item after item, and I recorded her final instructions on my trusty laptop.

Mom was a 5'2" glamour-puss who loved wearing fashionable high heels. Her family and friends knew this about her and often gave her gifts inspired by her shoe fetish. In fact she had a chair in the shape of a stiletto shoe, resplendent with leopard print upholstery, which my twenty-year old niece Briana now proudly owns. As Mom and I went through the bequeathal exercise we honed in on her curio cabinet filled with tiny objects of art. She assigned a crystal high heel to each of her granddaughters, but there remained a gold and red high heel lapel pin that seemed to have no new owner. For some bizarre reason Mom couldn't decide who should have it. I found this to be a curious thing as the woman was very opinionated about every other item we discussed. Finally she said, "Teeter, you can decide who to give this to. I trust you'll make the right decision."

A few months later Mom died. After the memorials were complete, I had the task of clearing out her home and distributing the remaining personal items. Jean helped me with this daunting, emotionally-charged task. She was one of Mom's primary caregivers and blessed to be with her when she died. After days of moving hundreds of items, I came upon the high heel pin, looked at the list to see to whom it should go and remembered it had no owner. I set it aside, waiting for the right answer to appear. A while later Jean suggested that we perform a burial ceremony of this precious item to honor the place where Mom took her last breath. Hers was an inspired idea.

In my mother's final weeks she would often stare out her bedroom window at the large oak tree and enjoy watching the birds at the birdfeeder. There was one bird in particular, a cardinal, who was her favorite. Every day the dazzling red bird would visit my mother. Mom would cheerfully say, "There's my friend again!" each time it would land on the branches. Right after she died the cardinal stopped coming around.

On the eve of the final move-out day, I had a hauntingly vivid dream where Mom was a cardinal flying around in her backyard. In my dream she landed on the ground and stayed in one particular spot near the hedges just to the left of the big oak tree. When Jean came over the next morning, I told her about my vision and said, "That's where we should bury Mom's pin." Within minutes a cardinal flew into the backyard and landed on the *exact spot* I had seen the night before. I was awe-struck by this 'coincidence' and felt a profound connection to both Mom and Spirit. Buoyed by the magic we had just witnessed, Jean and I immediately went outside and performed a touching little ceremony honoring my mother and this patch of Earth she occupied for a while.

Having Mom's glitzy pin buried in Mother Earth gives me comfort and peace knowing that some of her spirit remains in that space. Since then my mother frequently visits me as a cardinal; I often see or hear this colorful bird when I am thinking of her or needing support. Mom once promised me that she was intending to hover over her loved ones after she passed on and instructed me to watch for the signs. Every time I see the flashy red bird that flits around me a little longer than usual, I know my dear mother is keeping her promise.

Never Forget
From Whence You Came

I RECENTLY KNELT ON THE GROUND at the foot of my
mother's cemetery monument deep in the heart of the Midwestern plains. As she would have liked, her final tribute
was simple and heartfelt; the perfect ending to this phenomenal
woman's life.

Right after Mom's diagnosis, she wanted to get all of her affairs in
order as quickly as possible, intending to focus her remaining time
on more important things: sharing stories, laughing, praying, and
reconnecting with those whom she had not spoken in years. To
that end, on a sunny afternoon in late July Mom had the difficult
conversation with her children about what she wanted done with
her cremated remains.

Mom carefully considered her top two choices for inurnment:
Florida, where she had been living for many years, or South Dakota, her birthplace. Mom had been leaning towards the beauty
of the lush Florida landscape, but thanks to the sage advice of my
brother Doug, she ultimately decided that the connections to her
history, her ancestors, and the heartland were more important.
While Mom was decisive as to the cemetery plot and the style of

her monument—choosing a fancy black marble bench rather than a traditional headstone—she made it perfectly clear she wanted her children to decide what the inscription should be. She trusted us to find the words that were appropriate and reflective of the woman she was. I suspect that Mom's reticence to make this choice stemmed from her long-standing refusal to acknowledge the year of her birth. She was, after all, the woman who celebrated her forty-seventh birthday every year.

After her death my brothers and I finalized the plans for her snazzy inurnment bench. We decided on an elegant engraving of her name, dates of birth and death (Sorry, Ma!), and two quotes: "Don't grieve for me, for now I'm free" on one side, and "Never forget from whence you came" on the other. The former came from the memorial card she had selected, and the latter was a suggestion Allan had made. This second phrase was a familiar one; Mom often used it when she thought us kids were getting too hoity-toity for our own good. Through years of struggle my mom made the huge leap from poor Dakota girl living in a two-room house with no indoor plumbing, to a well-traveled, cosmopolitan woman living in a lovely home with all the creature comforts one could want. Even though her hard work resulted in a successful, rewarding career, she never forgot, nor wanted us to forget, her humble beginnings. She believed that only in a state of humility could true gratitude be expressed. It seemed fitting, therefore, that her ashes would rest for eternity in this simple cemetery carved from a South Dakota cornfield.

Since I am so connected with my mom's spirit I thought that visiting that place and her bench would be anticlimactic. However, as I walked closer to the bench, the lump in my throat grew bigger and my knees began to buckle. I saw her name—Kaylene Ann Hansen. I saw the dates—October 21, 1942 to November 28, 2006. The last date was more than mere letters and numbers etched in stone; it was the pivotal day that changed my life forever.

Mom had often visualized what that day would bring. She imagined she would die comfortably in her bed surrounded by family, music, candles, and photos of loved ones who could not be present. She anticipated a joyful reunion with those who had passed on before her and the magnificent return to the Light. Thanks to her prayers and the Grace of Spirit, her moment of transition was exactly as she had envisioned. When I said goodbye to her that night, I hugged her tightly, gazed at her smiling face, and watched with amazement as her spirit peacefully rose from her body, joining the angels waiting to accompany her. I was overwhelmed with joy and gratitude to Spirit for this moment, repeatedly wailing, "Thank you!", "Yes!" and "You did it, Mom!" at the top of my lungs. I didn't worry about who would hear my primal screams or what they would think. My tears were a mixture of sadness and deep appreciation. Mom had finally received what she had so fervently desired and for what the two of us had so often prayed. November 28th marked the day I went from *wanting to believe* that a Higher Power exists to *knowing* that It does.

Six months later I found myself sitting on the hard ground next to Mom's bench, quietly weeping and rubbing my fingertips gently over the letters, "Never forget from whence you came." I remembered many of Mom's stories from her childhood: decorating a Quaker oatmeal canister to make the majorette's hat she would don for the town parade, wearing old curtains to play dress-up with her sisters, and ripping pages from the Sears catalog for toilet paper in the family outhouse. I thought of the amazing things Mom did in her life and how much she accomplished. I thought of how much she taught me about courage, strength, perseverance, gratitude, and love.

As I stood in the whipping winds of the South Dakota prairie under a sky that stretched forever, I was not only thankful for the many gifts she bestowed during her time on Earth but also for those she continues to give from the Spirit World. Her love is constant and she provides me advice and support whenever I ask for it. Mom remains my greatest inspiration and I feel her powerful presence in my heart always.

Despite my deeply felt grief and the healing work that still lies ahead of me, I proudly proclaim that my mother's death was one of the most intense, wondrous experiences I have ever been blessed to witness. What a gift it was to watch her return to the place from whence she truly came! Thanks, Mom, for everything. I love you so much, and I'm glad you are finally back home.

THE YEAR OF FIRSTS

GRIEF HAS ITS OWN SPECIAL LANGUAGE. For example, all those who have experienced the death of a family member or close friend are familiar with The Year of Firsts. The Year of Firsts is that first full calendar year after loved ones have died where holidays, birthdays, anniversaries and other special days are observed without them. Since my mother's death I have experienced Mother's Day, Emma's birthday, and the anniversary of Mom's diagnosis. I recently lived through another difficult First: Mom's birthday. That was a tough one.

Her birthday this year was a sad one indeed. I ached to do what I had done every year prior; give her a big hug, wish her a happy birthday, present her with a thoughtful gift, and tell her how much I loved her. Instead, I spent the day immersed in grief, recalling a parade of memories and acutely feeling her absence. I shoveled fistfuls of cookies, crackers, and chocolate into my mouth because healthy foods held absolutely no appeal. But the warmth and fullness that junk food temporarily provided was no match to the crushing heaviness in my heart.

I remembered Mom's birthday one year ago; we all knew it was to be her last. She put up a good front, but it was obvious she was all but ready to let go. As I thought about her last birthday, I told myself that my mother wouldn't have wanted to live to see another one if she had to endure the pain and limitation that cancer brought with it. This rationale may have been true, but it provided little comfort.

Throughout the day I revisited the many details of Mom's journey including the initial acknowledgement of her condition, the process of teaching Emma about death, the late-night spiritual discussions on Mom's couch, the remarkable moment of her passing, and other highly emotional steps along the way. So many memories came flooding into my consciousness, all because of the date on the calendar.

Thankfully one mother helped me emerge from my depression over losing another. After wallowing in sorrow for hours, I went outdoors and into Mother Nature, lying on the ground under the late afternoon sky. As I breathed out my sadness into the Earth, I was suddenly aware of the strong roots from the nearby tree, the sun on my face, and the breeze on my body. The roots reminded me to ground my own energy into the Earth to become solid and secure once again, the sun helped me to recharge my batteries with life-affirming energy, and the wind lifted my heart, blowing away the heavy pall that was cast around me. The Earth was my healer, and Mom's spirit was right there waiting to guide me back to joy.

A few days earlier I told Emma that her grandmother's birthday was fast approaching. My daughter's tears revealed how much she missed her Mim. Yet in classic Emma fashion, she decided to celebrate Mom's birthday anyway and planned on sending her "an energy present." Only out of the mouths of babes could something so poignant, so perfect, spring forth. Just as she suggested, Emma and I lifted our outstretched arms into the sky on my mother's birthday and sent her an energy gift wrapped in a big, colorful ribbon of love.

I believe we are eternal beings with no beginning or end. When we die, we don't go away; we merely change form. While it's true I had the great privilege of witnessing my mother's transformation from the physical to the spiritual, I still experience the aching sadness of having said goodbye to her. This Year of Firsts and all subsequent milestones allow me to bathe in memories of times past, both joyful and painful. Yes, death marks the end of our physical lives. But at the same time, it marks the beginning of something sacred and magical to emerge.

The Divine spiral continues...

LIBERATION

"As we let our light shine, we consciously give other people permission to do the same. As we are liberated from our own fear, our presence actually liberates others."

—MARIANNE WILLIAMSON

A Rose
By Any Other Name

I WAS TRACY ROSE until two days ago. I legally changed my name to Theresa Rose on the first anniversary of my mother's death. Based on the reactions of some family members and friends, you'd think I pulled an Ozzy and bit the head off a bat. People typically respond with a mixture of shock, disbelief, confusion, and an occasional pinch of admiration. Who would have thought that going from Tracy to Theresa would be such a big deal?

The idea of changing my name initially came to me as I was finishing the book you are now holding. I was having a discussion with an author friend of mine and confessed to some reservations about having Tracy Rose as my by-line. I suggested the name of Theresa Rose—Theresa being the name I always secretly wanted growing up—and she thought it was perfect. From this brief, innocent conversation a new identity was born.

I could have easily used Theresa Rose as my pen name and kept Tracy Rose as my legal name. But the more I thought about it, the more I liked the idea of deep-sixing my birth name entirely in favor of adopting the new, exotic name of my childhood dreams. Before going off half-cocked just to fulfill some schoolgirl fantasy, I meditated for a long time to uncover my true feelings about my name and the motivation for changing it.

Through my meditations I discovered that I never felt comfortable as a Tracy. From my own goofy perspective the name struck me as the quintessential cheerleader name. Although I was, in fact, a wielder of pom-poms many moons ago, I no longer saw myself in that light. Tracy is inherently a perky name, and I am not a perky person. Intense, enthusiastic, passionate? Absolutely. Perky? Not so much. If I have a choice between a saint or a cheerleader as a namesake, I'm gonna go with the saint, thank you very much.

Another thing that had always annoyed me about my name was the fact that it's one of those unisex names given to both girls and boys. Nothing was more aggravating than meeting or reading about a guy named Tracy. Ugh. Let's see if I can feel any more unattractive. (Please forgive me if your name is Tracy, Chris or Pat; I'm sure you are a lovely man or woman.)

As evidence of the total mismatch of my name to my personality, I can cite on one hand the number of people in my personal life who actually call me by my birth name. In the professional world, students and clients often refer to me as Ms. Rose. I'm not deluding myself into thinking that it is done solely out of deference. Most likely the formal moniker is due to their natural resistance to the aforementioned perkiness of my name. Nearly everyone in my family and many of my closest friends call me T, Teeter, or Trace. Even my dear spouse has called me by his favorite nickname since our early dating days. (He forbade me from including it here.) I have been called many things over the years but Tracy is rarely one of them.

Given these circumstances, I felt certain the transition from Tracy to Theresa would be smooth. When I started telling people about my decision, I was surprised at the mild uproar that ensued. It wasn't because they couldn't see me as Theresa since the name seemed to fit. While most people understood the reasons for the name change, many found it unsettling that I was actually going through with it.

The messages behind the perplexed looks and seemingly innocent questions were obvious. People aren't supposed to change their names willy-nilly! It doesn't matter if you don't like your name; it was the name you were given and, dammit, you should accept it! What will everyone think? Won't you disappoint your family? Aren't you too old to go changing your name now? Who do you think you are?

Many of us were taught as children that we should suck it up when things don't go our way. If we don't like something, we learn to muffle our negative emotions, do our best to ignore them, and hope they will dissipate over time. As adults, when our unhappy thoughts and feelings don't simply fade into the mist, we mask our disappointment, pain or anger with food, booze, drugs, shopping, sex, television or some other anesthetic. We remain victims of our circumstances for years because we are too afraid or too numb to do anything about them.

I decided to become Theresa Rose to reclaim the power of my name, and I specifically chose the momentous anniversary of my mother's death as my new birth-day. She consciously transitioned to Spirit, and I am consciously transitioning to Theresa. I have to say, I love my new name! I love what it means, how it sounds, and how it makes me feel. The word comes from the Greek word *therizein* meaning harvest. Theresa is "one who reaps", a person who works hard and will surely receive great rewards for her efforts. I like that; it suits me.

Most importantly, changing my name became a symbol of the transformation I have undergone over the last year. As I say goodbye to Tracy, I also say goodbye to her limitations and fears. As I welcome Theresa into my world, I open myself up to huge new possibilities for joy, prosperity, and growth. By filling out some forms and forking-over a few hundred bucks, I liberated myself from a lifelong sense of not-quite-right while gaining a strong new identity and a kick-ass by-line. Theresa Rose symbolizes who I am now, what I want to accomplish moving forward, and how I can confidently live my truth without allowing the opinions of others to change my self-image. This is a wonderful time of blossoming for this particular Rose, and I am proud of the gutsy decision I made to make a few simple changes in lettering.

We are living in times of great discovery and change. If you are like me and don't feel connected to your birth name, change it. If you don't like the way your life is unfolding, change it. There is nothing happening to you that you aren't allowing. We are never too old or too set in our ways to change course if we so choose. Let's be like butterflies emerging from our cocoons and spread our gorgeous wings. It's time to fly!

Embracing What Is

ɞ

I'M TOYING AROUND with the idea of sponsoring a local Overachievers Anonymous chapter meeting. Folks like me could meet weekly to discuss our obsessions du jour and the various ways we torture ourselves in the futile attempt at perfection. Come to think of it, maybe the meetings should be held twice a week so we can get more done.

My twelve-step confession would sound something like this: "Hello. My name is Theresa, and I am an overachiever. (Hi, Theresa!) I am powerless over my lifelong addiction to please. I don't quit until a project is done flawlessly. I go above and beyond what is reasonable and healthy. I keep going when others fail or give up. I work as long as it takes. I'm a machine, and like a machine, I don't know when to stop. I keep blindly marching, marching, marching toward the finish line. This addiction has made me ill and robbed me of the ability to appreciate the special things in my life."

My addiction started at a young age and was a constant presence throughout my years in school. Being a model student, my grades were exemplary and my extracurricular activities were varied and numerous. I earned accolades in academics, drama, student government, and community service. My mother used to refer to my bedroom as "The Shrine" since the walls and shelves were covered with awards, ribbons, and plaques honoring my various achievements. Yeah, I was one of *those* kids.

The lone tick mark on my scholastic resume was my freshman year in high school when I tried on the identity of slacker chick. Other than my brief stumble down Burnout Lane, I enjoyed learning and eagerly devoured my studies. However, my academic motivation was not only to satisfy my appetite for knowledge, but also to enjoy the sweet nectar of recognition.

When I came bounding home toting an A+ paper, my mother would say, "Teeter, I would expect nothing less." While her response was well-intentioned, it felt like a back-handed compliment. Instead of making me feel good, her proclamation only reinforced my determination to do even better next time. (If there was such as thing as an A++ to be earned, then I wanted it.) A simple "Great job, Honey!" was all I really wanted to hear. I convinced myself that if I worked a little harder, accomplished a little more, and earned a better grade, I would get the appreciation I desperately craved and happiness would quickly follow. Through my own eyes, nothing I ever did was noteworthy, good enough, or cause for celebration.

This emotional disease continued unabated well beyond graduation day. Once I joined the workforce I worked my fingers to the bone, aggressively sprinting up the professional ladder. Instead of receiving plaques for my superhuman efforts, I received promotions. (If I could have displayed them, I would have.) It was during this time that I started to experience the physical affects of my need to please. I had frequent headaches, ulcers, acne, grinding teeth, back pain and hair loss, not to mention a serious food addiction and the resultant lower-than-dirt self-esteem. My need to excel laid an internal minefield of unrealistic expectations where fear, depression, anger, and panic regularly exploded within me.

The most tragic consequence of my unquenchable desire to succeed has been my near-manic fixation on what *will be*, causing me to totally lose sight of what *is*. I've missed out on fully enjoying the many fruits of my labor, both big and small, because part of me was preoccupied with getting to The Next Big Thing. While this neurotic tendency proved highly beneficial to former employers, it effectively stole much of my life from me.

But no more. It is time for me to exit the Waiting Room From Hell where I have been busy waiting, hoping, wishing, planning, and dreaming my days away. I want to liberate myself from my needless pursuit of the illusory end-zone so I can finally start enjoying the ride.

People don't wait in line for the Splash Mountain roller coaster at DisneyWorld because they think they'll have a rotten time. They go on it because it's fun! When they are climbing up the first peak, they are not thinking about the next attraction they'll visit, nor are they trying to dictate the speed or direction the cars will take. While strapped in, they expect to be dazzled, willingly relinquish control, and trust that they'll be safe at all times. The expected adrenaline rush is why they step onto the platform in the first place. Even though they know the ride will come to an end, they hop aboard anyway for the thrill of the moment.

Life is like Splash Mountain but so much better. It's like an amusement park ride, skydiving jump, white-water rafting, and hot, sweaty sex all rolled into one. Yet through social, educational, and parental conditioning, we often forget the fun and treat it like one long IRS audit. This forgetfulness is at the root of my over-achievement addiction. I kept thinking that my life will get better when x, y, or z happens instead of drinking in the beauty of the Now. When I unplug, look around and appreciate the magnificence all around me—big poofy clouds in a crystal-blue sky, a hawk sailing in the afternoon breeze, a white rose in full-bloom, my daughter's smile—my futuresightedness magically corrects itself and I happily land in the present.

It's probable that a not-yet-attained accolade will dance in front of me in the future, causing my overachievement addiction to resurface. When that happens, I hope I can remember to embrace what is instead of obsessing over what will be. I have learned that there is only one finish line, and none of us will cross it until we cross over. Through my own choice, I am on the ride of my life and securely buckled in. There aren't any plaques or promotions that are worth more than enjoying this very moment, right now.

Calgon,
Take Me Away!

⌘

I AM TEETER. This childhood nickname was originally given to me because my first name starts with the letter T. Over time the name took on a new, less cheery meaning. Teeter stuck because of my tendency to swing back and forth on an emotional see-saw from ecstasy to angst, from exhilaration to exhaustion. As a senior in high school I was elected the President of the Drama Club, embodying the role as much offstage as on. There was always some real-life drama just over the horizon that gave me yet another opportunity to Teeter.

My cycle of peaks and valleys has stayed with me throughout adulthood. I still struggle to stay happy while providing for my family, managing a career, keeping our home in moderately presentable fashion, maintaining friendships, and finding a teensy-weensy bit of personal time. If I don't take time to recharge my batteries, I can easily turn into an anger ball or a mopey baby in no time. Most often my mood swings are caused by old habits, a lack of grounding, raging hormones or insane expectations I place on myself. It seems I am constantly chasing the Holy Grail known as The Balanced Life. Isn't that what we all want? Don't we all want to feel in the groove regardless of what is happening around us?

Even when things are coasting along smoothly, something insignificant can rock my world and I'll have another one of my Teeter episodes. Suddenly everything I do takes twice as long as it normally does, my temper flares over the silliest things, and tears flow for "no good reason." The most frequent excuse I use to justify my occasional meltdowns is PMS, the monthly visitor that often wreaks havoc in the Rose household. (Michael does get a wee bit suspicious, however, when I invoke premenstrual freak-out privileges four or five times in the same month.) While my teetering sounds slightly schizophrenic, I don't believe I suffer from any sort of psychological disorder, at least none that require immediate hospitalization.

Regardless of the reason, whether it is hormonally-influenced or not, we all have bad days where we want to put on a hockey helmet, cower in the corner in a fetal position, and bawl our eyes out for seventy-two hours. But we don't. We keep going. We believe we *have* to keep going because the people we love are counting on us. Because of this martyrdom, most of us try to gut it out instead of honoring our feelings and the need to check out for a while. We keep plugging away even though we have run out of gas. Eventually we experience an out-of-nowhere emotional eruption akin to Mount Vesuvius, spewing nastiness all over our unfortunate families and friends. Had we just admitted that we were at wit's end and addressed our needs in the first place, we could have spared everyone our verbal blitzkrieg.

Paradoxically, the healthiest response to my hockey helmet moments is to quickly relinquish the crown of the perfect working woman/wife/mother. Sometimes maintaining a sense of balance means accepting my humanity and giving myself permission to receive that which I truly need the most—nurturing.

During those Teeter times, I allow myself generous servings of prima donna pampering. Whatever action feels downright extravagant is what I do. Whether it's walking on the beach on a warm summer's day, sneaking out to catch a matinee of the latest Johnny Depp movie (bringing plenty of napkins to wipe the drool from my chin), getting a full-body massage, or simply taking a sweet-smelling bubble bath, I shower some much-needed attention on my frantic, frazzled soul. It is nothing short of remarkable what can result from a brief stay in the luxurious world of self-care. When I turn off my computer, silence the ringer on my cell phone, light candles and incense, and step into a lavender bubble bath I can soak away almost any worry and resume human form in less than a half-hour. Joy returns as my welcome companion and Teeter has left the building. Mission accomplished.

Many of us have been taught that recognizing and honoring our own needs is a selfish act. Little voices in our heads tell us we don't deserve to give attention to ourselves or that it is unseemly to do so. On the contrary, I believe that nurturing myself is a conscious, deliberate choice that ultimately serves everyone in my life. The phrase "self-serving" is usually used to negatively describe some-one or something. But what is wrong with serving oneself when it enhances our ability to serve others? We can liberate ourselves from the self-imposed prisons of swinging moods and unnecessary anguish quite simply: by finally releasing the role of martyr, rais-ing the white flag of surrender, and indulging in some good old fashioned TLC. Achieving balance is within our grasp when we remember to love ourselves, knowing that it is one of the most self-less acts we can perform. Be honest; you know that making dinner can wait, writing that last e-mail can wait, and sorting laundry can wait. This is *your* time. So what are you waiting for? Start running the bath water!

VICTIMGIRL

N O MATTER HOW MANY self-help books I read, healing workshops I attend, or meditations I practice, I have yet to rid myself entirely of Victimgirl. She is the crabby, obnoxious little voice inside my head who tells me how freakin' hard life is. Victimgirl has been within me for as long as I can remember, and I am doing my best to liberate myself from her emotional grip.

Victimgirl is the eternal pessimist who sees everything in her world as difficult. To her, life is a series of obstacles and disappointments instead of the delicious, rich adventure that it is. She can take simple, everyday facets of life and twist them around so they seem more arduous, painful, or odious than they really are. The language she speaks is peppered with have-tos, got-tos, need-tos, should-haves, and musts. Arghh!! Enough already. It's time for her to put a sock in it.

Victimgirl shows up most frequently on Sunday afternoons. It is at this time when my masochism kicks into overdrive. As a wife and mom, I have several domestic tasks to do on the weekend in order for my family to be ready and rarin' to go when Monday rolls around. Rarely do I wake up on Sunday mornings without automatically dreading the upcoming household duties of the day. You'd think I would have gotten used to the routine after living with it for over a decade. Yet every Sunday I start my weekly temper tantrum about two o'clock in the afternoon. I get bitchy. I start slamming stuff around. I stop being nice to my husband and daughter and start adopting the "poor, poor, pitiful me" attitude.

If Michael oh-so-gingerly suggests that I temporarily put aside some of my chores so I may enjoy the rest of my weekend (and he can enjoy the rest of his), Victimgirl arrives on the scene with a vengeance. She scowls at him and whines, "I can't! Don't you understand? I *have* to get this stuff done *right now*!" while she angrily puts the last of the newly-scrubbed lunch plates onto the dish drainer. The silver lining of Black Sundays is the weekly lovemaking romps with Michael. By some freakish twist of fate he actually still wants to have sex with me after witnessing my tirades all afternoon. Hmmm...maybe *he's* the masochist.

My Ms. Hyde routine has brought with it not only the unpleasantness of my poor-me drama, but also the bitter aftertaste of guilt. If I catch myself blah-blah blahing about the oh-so-heavy burdens I carry, I'll eventually get a major case of the guilts when I think about how incredible my life *really* is compared to how rough things are for so many others. Just a few words and images will jolt me out of my pity party and remind me of what a selfish prick I am being. The genocide in Darfur, the tragedy of sick and hungry babies, and the horrors of war would make my silly-ass complaints about laundry seem laughable if they weren't so pathetic. Despite my mental walks of shame, I still find myself morphing into a whiny-baby nearly every week.

Unfortunately this habit isn't limited to weekend domestic activities. I can change into Victimgirl when I'm getting ready to take a trip ("I have all this packing to do!"), when schlepping my daughter to her after-school activities ("I need to get Em to Karate right away!"), or even when something exciting is happening ("I have to get ready for my meditation workshop!"). When I'm in the vicious cycle of martyrdom, I run around like the proverbial chicken with its head cut off, angrily jumping from task to task. Smiles are rare sightings when VG is in the house.

After everything I have experienced in my thirty-eight years I have come to the conclusion that I don't want to live with this part of me anymore. It simply doesn't *feel* good to be this bitchy. Like George Bailey, I want to be more grateful for and appreciative of my wonderful life. Since my early days of depressed drama queen, I've made leaps and bounds towards the Land of the Conscious. Yet I still have so much more work to do. When will I be completely free from the shackles of oughta-gotta-musta? If my mother's death taught me anything, it was this: life is a precious gift not to be squandered. It's time for me to stop acting in my personal theatre of the absurd where every day is some nightmare to endure.

A therapist friend of mine recently gave me some great advice on how to shed my Victimgirl persona. She suggested that I give voice to my masochistic side instead of relegating it to scowls, slammed doors and furrowed brows. By talking to my inner victim and hearing how much she doesn't want to do something, I end up discovering the truth underneath the tantrums. This process of deconstructing my whine-fests has gotten me back to Happy Theresa a whole lot faster.

Here's how the dialogue often begins. As I feel the familiar burning in my stomach when some loathsome chore beckons—going to the grocery store, for example—I stop what I'm doing and go into another room. I ask Victimgirl if she really wants to go to the grocery store and let her respond as loudly and bitchy as she wants. She shouts, "No I don't want to go to that horrible place! It's so busy, and it will take forever! I don't have the energy to go! Why do I have to do it? This sucks!!!" (Yep, I actually say these things out loud.) Victimgirl gets to say as much as she wants, as bitchy as she wants, until there is simply no more bitch left in her.

Then I say to her, "Wow. That sounds excruciating. I don't blame you for not wanting to go. What is the consequence of not going to the store right now?" She responds by saying that we wouldn't have

184

any food to make our meals for the week. As a follow-on question I ask, "is that an acceptable alternative for you?" She thinks about it for a moment and eventually responds quietly in the negative. Finally I ask her, "So, are you *choosing* to go to the grocery store instead of *having* to go?" After mulling it over the answer she provides is short and sweet; "Yeah, I guess I am." This simple exercise minimizes my victimhood and places conscious Theresa back in the driver's seat where she belongs.

My solution may seem a bit wacky and overly dramatic, but hey, it works for me. (Don't forget that I *am* a former President of the Drama Club.) By recognizing and unplugging from this self-destructive program, allowing my inner whiner to complain as loudly as possible, identifying my alternatives, and ultimately admitting that I choose everything I do, I have been able to minimize the sightings of Victimgirl.

Unfortunately my role-playing therapy is by no means a fail-proof solution. In order for my theatrics to stand a chance at success I must first be made aware that I've come down with a case of the Uglies. (This is one of the handy benefits of having a loving, compassionate family nearby.) Yet even more critical to its success is to admit that I *want* to stop feeling like a martyr. I confess that this penchant for pain has served me over the years. It has made me feel safe, valued, and deserving of the many gifts bestowed upon me.

For years I thought that life shouldn't be too good, or more precisely, my response to it shouldn't be too high-spirited. If so, God would punish my self-indulgence and snatch away those things that made me happy in the first place. If I complain loudly enough, then maybe Spirit won't take anything special away from me. If I work like a crazy woman, then maybe my husband and daughter will give me some extra love and attention. If I struggle, then maybe I'll earn more respect from family, friends and co-workers. These are but some of the nutty ways I subconsciously rationalized my bad behavior. By looking at what is underneath the masochism I start to do the real work of addressing my insecurities. I am learning to ask for what I want and need, trust that Spirit provides abundance in every way, and ultimately allow myself unbridled joy and prosperity.

I believe we have chosen, allowed, or promoted all of our experiences, either actively or by default. We have chosen our homes, our jobs, our partners, our friends, our moods, and every other aspect of our lives—no exceptions. We have even chosen to be victims of our circumstances every once in a while. Once we really get the fact that we don't *have* to do anything we truly don't *want* to do, we can start enjoying the party a little more. It's pretty simple really. Life can be hard or life can be joyful. The choice is ours to make.

Finding God
in the Dining Room

S OME PEOPLE FIND GOD on a mountaintop. Many find
Him in a house of worship. Still others find Him while
visiting sacred sites or making a pilgrimage around the
world. I found Him in the dining room.

Well, it used to be a dining room. Now it's something completely
different. When people visit our home, they immediately encoun-
ter God Central, our carefully appointed sacred haven designed
exclusively for all things spiritual. Our choice to have a meditation
room instead of a dining room may seem goofy to some, but its
presence allows us to have a dose of the Divine Mojo at any time
of the day or night.

Michael and I turned our domestic floor plan on its ear several years ago when our daughter started toddling. It seemed silly
to have a fancy-schmancy, unused dining room while at the same
time being in desperate need of more practical living space. Bucking convention, we ditched our formal dining area and replaced it
with a charming little playroom complete with Emma-sized furniture and other pre-school sundries.

However, the playroom was not to remain. We soon realized that

Emma didn't want to be anywhere where her parents were not. If we were in the kitchen, then Emma would be twirling and sliding all over the tile floor. If we were in our bedroom, then she'd be jumping on the bed and jibber-jabbering to anyone who would listen. Since neither of her parents favored sitting on uncomfortable Romper Room chairs for more than a few minutes at a time, the luster of the playroom quickly wore off. The playroom followed the familiar path of the dining room and became a dusty, ignored section of valuable domestic real estate.

When Michael and I expanded our spiritual practice a few years ago to include yoga, daily prayer, sound healing, and energy work, it seemed only natural to convert the playroom into a meditation room. After removing all traces of kiddie-land, we set about making our very first sacred space. After months of iterative changes, we ended up with a super-charged room containing an elaborate altar, pictures of righteous spiritual teachers and heroes, crystals, drums, feathers, rattles, yoga mats, meditation pillows and oodles of other spiritual accoutrements. It's our own private place of worship.

When we first created our special room, I was totally freaked-out at the thought of other people evaluating it. "Will the neighbors think we're nuts?", "Will they ridicule our spiritual beliefs?" and "Will we be ostracized?" were unspoken questions I frequently asked of myself when the sun went down. As evenings drew near, I would hurriedly close the blinds to shield our sacred space from the inquisitive eyes of local dog-walkers. I feared they would judge me for doing Reiki, shoulderstands and ecstatic dance in the room typically used to serve the Thanksgiving turkey.

Most first-time visitors to the sacred room get a skosh confused by it. After all, it's not every day one walks into someone's home and finds gongs, crystal bowls, piles of rocks, dried herbs and condor feathers (at least in this country). One's typical reaction is to either nervously avoid the room entirely or blankly stare at it with that recognizable deer-in-the-headlights look. Only my teenage niece had the spunk to say, "Auntie, walk me through this. What does it all mean?" It was a refreshing thing to be asked directly about my spiritual practice instead of having it ignored or quietly judged.

Admittedly our collection of sacred objects may strike some as bizarre. We possess an unusual combination of artifacts from Christianity, Hinduism, Buddhism, and Shamanism among others. Come to think of it, that combo would be a fair characterization of our flavor of spirituality. Contrary to what some members of my family may think or fear, I'm not stabbing voodoo dolls or drinking goat's blood. Like them, I am simply connecting to God in the way that feels right to me.

In order for me to fully engage my relationship with Spirit on a daily basis, I had to let go of old personal fears which tried to convince me that one way of devotion was right and all other ways were wrong. I came to believe that Spirit is like a huge tent of love underneath which everyone can fit in peace and harmony. All of humanity can choose to attend the Divine barbeque if they so choose. There may be some folks eating bratwursts, others enjoying corn on the cob, and a small gathering on lawn chairs eating their franks and beans. Everyone is at the same party, yet they are all experiencing it a little differently. Each person can have a great time, especially if none of the partygoers forces their choices on the rest of the gang. Just because people have different preferences at the Divine barbeque doesn't make them wrong and me right or vice versa. We're just different. I like to think that was part of the plan.

My spiritual liberation came when I decided to honor the opinions of others who may judge my spiritual practice rather than perceiving their views as personal attacks. While our approach may be a tad unorthodox, I fully support those whose spiritual leanings tend toward the traditional. If following an organized religion is your thing, go for it! If creating your own brand of spirituality suits you better, that's great too. The details of one's practice aren't ultimately what matters; rather it's the authenticity and depth of one's connection to the Creator that is paramount.

My daily communion in our meditation room helps me experience genuine peace and joy that only regular spiritual practice can bring. No matter the nature of your spiritual affiliation, I invite you to create a sacred space in your home that helps you honor and connect with Spirit in your own way. It can be a room, a dresser, a shelf, or a patch of ground. It can be by the book or off-the-cuff. The aesthetics of one's sacred space aren't what's important, it's the intention behind it. Dedicating some small part of our hectic world to holy pursuits can lighten our daily load and promote deeper healing. I personally don't believe we need to go across the street, downtown or across the globe to find God. Its Loving Presence is with us whoever we are, wherever we are. Always.

OPENING YOUR
OWN KIMONO

S
O NOW YOU KNOW some of my secrets. I should be
mortified at the thought of strangers knowing my life's
most intimate details. I suppose I would be if it weren't for
this fact: my emotional exhibitionism transformed me. I have experienced hundreds of hours of healing work over the years, from
traditional psychotherapy to Kundalini yoga to Native American
sweat lodges, and nothing has come close to the life-changing shifts
that occurred through the cathartic act of opening my kimono. Finally I am free of the self-inflicted emotional straitjacket.

If you are like me—recovering from a loss, undergoing a major
life change, or simply struggling to find some measure of health,
balance, and peace while living in an increasingly stressful world—
I encourage you to do what I did: start documenting your stories.
Use a journal, computer, tape recorder, or cocktail napkin. Use
anything that will help you speak your truth. Fess up; you've always secretly thought your life story would make a great book,
right? Right!

Once you've recorded your stories, choose a time to share them
with loved ones and friends. Tell them about your trials and tribu-

lations and the progress you are making in overcoming them. Be sure to give attention to the juicy lessons you learned and the gifts you received. While it may be tempting, don't leave out any of the ugly stuff! You will feel so liberated once you expose who you really are to those special people in your world. Remember that the truth is always a good thing; it really will set you free.

The stories you have just read are unique to me, but their themes are universal. Both you and I have felt pain, judged ourselves too harshly, made a few cringe-worthy choices, and really just wanted to be loved. I believe our mission here on Earth is not to rid ourselves of human frailties altogether; rather it is to become aware of them, own them, learn from them, and ultimately embrace them. By doing so, these perceived imperfections might bring about our greatest transformations.

Navigating this scary new terrain of naked truth can be daunting. However, it gets easier the more one cultivates a deep relationship with one's Higher Power. If you are new to the spiritual realm, you may not know where to begin. Rest assured, getting to know Spirit doesn't have to be complicated; simply imagine you are establishing a new friendship. The foundation of every relationship is communication, and your growing connection with the Divine is no different.

See Spirit as your new best friend—call Him/Her regularly (through your quiet mind), talk about your latest and greatest happenings, and ask for advice or help when you need it. Learn about the spiritual world by asking questions and waiting for the answers to appear in signs, symbols, or "coincidences". It doesn't matter whether your conversations take place in a house of worship or in your own bathtub, nor does it matter whether you refer to them as prayer, meditation, or cosmic chitchat. The mechanics of your heavenly dialogue aren't what's important; rather, it is the energy and intention behind your thoughts and words that create a powerful union.

You will soon discover an infinite source of healing and guidance at your disposal whenever and wherever you need it. Your Divine Best Friend will always be there for you. He/She will never go on vacation, screen your calls, get too busy, move away, or die. Once you get on board the Spirit Train, you will quickly feel the comfort of knowing that you are never, *ever*, alone.

So pack your bags and start down your own healing path. With courage and determination, name those shadowy areas you wish to bring into the light. Attract the teachers, books, classes, and healing practitioners that will support you. Join your favorite local community of spiritual seekers. Know that you have the strength to open your own kimono. Acknowledge the beautiful, Divine being that lies beneath. Be vulnerable! Surrender! Trust!

I honor you. I believe in you.

CLUB KIMONO
DISCUSSION STARTERS

B Y NOW YOU KNOW that an honest expression of one's feelings and experiences can be a powerful agent of change. In order to help you begin to open your own kimono, I have provided some evocative questions for you to consider. Each question invites you to reflect on the stories in *Opening the Kimono* as well as gently coax you to start telling your own. Whether you are participating in a book club event or are a member of an ongoing Club Kimono discussion group in your area, these questions will get you thinking about your own colorful tapestry, spark animated and often hilarious discussions, and help guide you to express that which is uniquely you. For more information on hosting or locating a Club Kimono group near you, please visit www.clubkimono.net.

So, what's really going on underneath that kimono of yours? Isn't time to start exposing your beautiful self?

BODY

1. What was your favorite story in the Body section and why? What aspects of the author's experience resonated with you?

2. Was there anything in the stories that the author said or did that made you uncomfortable? Dive deeper into your negative reaction to uncover any programs, judgments, or fears that may be lurking.

3. What are your earliest memories of body image and weight?

4. Who were your heroes and role models growing up? How did their body image affect you?

5. Do you know how much you weigh right now? Do you care? If you know, do you judge the number as either too low or too high?

6. What is your relationship with your body? Is it revered or ignored? Do you see it as Divine or a disaster? To whom are you comparing it?

7. What is your relationship to food? Have you always enjoyed food without guilt? Do you view food as an energy provider, or does it soothe your emotions as well? Which foods are your favorite emotional salves and why?

8. What is your relationship with exercise and movement? Do you enjoy moving your body, and in what ways do you move it? If you do not, why? What are the rationalizations, excuses or judgments that quickly come to mind to keep you from joyfully moving your body?

9. Do you like to dance? If so, how often do you take the opportunity to dance? Have you ever danced around the house? What are your favorite dance tunes? How does the act of dancing make you feel? Why don't you do it more often?

10. Are there any addictions you currently have or have had in the past? How and when was your addiction born? If your addiction were an animal, what would it be and how would it behave?

LOVE & SEX

1. What was your favorite story in the Love & Sex section and why? What emotions surfaced as you read it? Did it motivate you in any way?

2. How do you feel about sex? How did you emotionally react to reading about it in such an open way?

3. What lessons and images do you recall from your childhood about sex? How would you describe your initial impressions of sex? How have these colored your current opinion of it?

4. What was your experience of puberty? What were memorable moments that have stayed with you all these years?

5. What are three words that describe your first sexual encounters?

6. What risks have you taken in relationships? Did those risks turn out to be a blessing or a curse? Was there a risk you didn't take and now look back on it as a missed opportunity?

7. What type of arguer are you? Who or where did you learn it from? How does it serve you and/or hurt you?

8. Who or what makes you jealous? How do you act when the green-eyed monster rears its ugly head? What fears lie underneath your jealousy?

9. Describe your perfect mate. Is this person in your life right now? If so, have you shared that information with him or her lately? If not, are you actively attracting him or her to you? In what ways?

10. Have you ever taken someone you love for granted? In what ways did you do so, and what were the consequences of your choices?

RAISING KIDS

1. What was your favorite story in the Kids section and why? What emotions surfaced as you read it? Did it motivate you in any way?

2. If you are a mom, what was your pregnancy like? If you are not, what are some recollections of pregnancies from friends or loved ones? What were the best parts and the most challenging parts?

3. What role did fear play in your own upbringing? Was safety a major factor in the way your parents raised you? How has this impacted you?

4. Did you grow up watching a lot of television? What were your favorite shows or movies? When looking back on your childhood TV time, what emotions does it elicit?

5. What foods did you eat as a child? How did that affect your adult diet? If you are a parent, has it affected how you provide for your family?

6. What's the phrase your parents used to say when you got into trouble? How do you feel about that phrase now? Do you say something similar to your own children?

7. In your view, what was the poorest choice your parents made when raising you? Can you understand why they made it at the time? If not, is it something you want to be able to eventually understand and work through?

8. If you are a parent, what is one thing you've said or done to your child that you wish you could take back? How can you make that right?

9. Did you have a diary or journal as a child? If so, what role did it serve for you? If not, was there another outlet for you to share your innermost feelings, like a stuffed animal, a best friend, or a pen pal?

10. Think of a special child in your life. If you observe the way that he or she lives, what valuable lessons can you learn from this little teacher?

CAREER

1. What was your favorite story in the Career section and why? What emotions surfaced as you read it? Did it motivate you in any way?

2. What careers did your parents or guardians have when you were growing up? Did they enjoy their careers? What are your feelings about those jobs? What did their opinions of their careers teach you?

3. What is your dream job? Describe it in rich detail, including how you will feel having it. Is there any reason other than fear that you aren't pursuing your dream?

4. What were your favorite jobs and why?

5. What were your least favorite jobs and why? What were the gifts in them?

6. What are the most important benefits of having your career other than to earn money? Are those benefits keeping you satisfied? If not, what can you do to change your situation?

7. How have you compared yourself to others in the working world? How has this comparison affected you emotionally?

8. Have you ever witnessed the Beauty or the Beast archetypes in your line of work? How do you feel about each role? Have you ever worked for one? Are you one yourself?

9. Who is your hero in the professional world and why? What skills does he or she possess that you don't believe you have? Name three specific things you can do to gain that knowledge and/or experience.

10. What professional successes and failures have you had? How did the so-called 'failures' eventually serve you?

DEATH

1. What was your favorite story in the Death section and why? What emotions surfaced as you read it? Did it motivate you in any way?

2. What was the first memory you have of death? How was the concept of death treated in your family?

3. What is the most amazing experience of death you have been blessed to witness, if any? What were the gifts you received?

4. How would you like your death to be? Who and what will be surrounding you? What do you think it will look and feel like at the moment of transition?

5. Describe your perfect funeral/celebration. What phrase would you want engraved on your monument?

6. If you were to die tomorrow, what is one thing you would regret not having done? Is there someone with whom you have an unresolved conflict? Is there any reason why you are choosing not to fix it now?

7. Do you have a spiritual relationship with someone special who has died? In what ways are they still present in your life? How do they "speak" to you or make themselves known? How does it make you feel when they visit? If you don't have a relationship with them in spirit, why?

8. What songs make you weep and why? Do you have a recording of them? If so, how often do you listen to them? If not, why?

9. If you were able to come back as an animal after you die, what would you choose and why? Who would you want to occasionally check on?

10. What do you think happens when you die? Are you comfortable with that image? Are you able to allow others to have opinions that may be different than yours? If not, why?

LIBERATION

1. What was your favorite story in the Liberation section and why? What emotions surfaced as you read it? Did it motivate you in any way?
2. How do you feel about your name? What do others call you? Do you have any nicknames? If you could have any other name in the world, what would it be and why? What ways can you incorporate some of the energy of that fantasy name into your life?
3. Would you describe yourself as having a balanced life? Why or why not? What nurturing activities do you do for yourself? If you rarely do anything for yourself, why do you perceive that to be less important than other activities?
4. Where in your life are you choosing to be a masochist? In what ways does it present itself? What are the catalysts? How does masochism serve you? How does it hurt you?
5. When was the last martyr freak-out you had and how did you feel while in the middle of it? How do you think your body physically reacted to it? How did others respond?
6. Do you have a sacred space in your home? If so, describe it. What makes it sacred to you? If you don't have one yet, do you want to create one? What would you choose to include in your sacred space? What would it look like?
7. What is your relationship to the Divine? How do you experience it? Is it a part of your daily life? If not, why? What ways can you incorporate more spirit into your world?
8. Is there any healing work that is calling out for you?
9. What is one big, ugly thing you have done that you are ready to release? Will you write it all down, even if it is initially only for your eyes to read? What immediate steps can you take to begin to share your stories with another?
10. What lessons did you ultimately take away from reading *Opening the Kimono*? What ways, if any, do you perceive yourself differently after reading the book?

ACKNOWLEDGMENTS

W RITING A BOOK is much like giving birth, and squeezing out this little bambina required lots of midwives. It would not have come to fruition had I not received major amounts of love, support, wisdom and guidance from many special people.

Thanks to the staff at Positive Change Media for providing me with my first opportunity to publicly share my truth.

Deep appreciation goes out to Barbara Harris Whitfield for selflessly sharing her writing experiences with me and providing a handy mental roadmap to the often-rocky terrain of becoming an author.

I am indebted to the thousands of clients, Reiki students, and meditation participants I have been lucky enough to meet over the years who allowed me to witness their inspiring journeys.

Much-deserved credit goes to the artistic visionaries who helped me to realize the gorgeous manifestation of *Opening the Kimono*. Heartfelt thanks goes to John Reinhardt for his impeccable book layout, Jack Davis for his killer cover design, Stephanie Dubsky for her beautiful headshot photographs, Elsie Gilmore for her outstanding work on my web site, Mark Zampella for his deft handling of the audiobook recording, and Wayne Eastep for creating the perfect image that captures the powerful essence of *Kimono*. Thank you, Wayne, for bringing my vision into delicious, full-color reality.

I am very blessed to have received so much compassionate healing work from many highly-skilled practitioners over the years. There are a few extra-special healers who were instrumental in helping me to find my personal power. They are Terry Schibler, Shaun Dumas, Sonie Lasker, and most of all, my dear friend and confidante Robert Byrne.

I humbly honor my spiritual teachers Betty Labbate, Dell Dell'Armo, Ruben Orellana, Kristen White, Jyoti, the Thirteen Indigenous Grandmothers, Chuck and Ashley Wile and all of the instructors at the Center for Sacred Studies. I would especially like to thank Anodea Judith, the Grande Dame of Chakras, and Frannie Hoffman, a true angel on Earth, for eloquently teaching me what nasty emotional gunk lurked in my dark corners and lovingly helping me to remove it.

Deep appreciation goes out to my entire family, especially my brothers Allan and Doug and my niece Briana Picotte, for understanding my need to share my stories so that others may heal.

I owe my life as a writer to three righteous women: Jean McManis, my best friend and muse; Susan Picotte, my soul sister and consiglieri; and Lourdes Ramirez, my spiritual guidance counselor. They selflessly served as my sounding boards, cheerleaders, advisors and confessors. Ladies, you rock.

Words alone cannot fully convey my overwhelming and heartfelt gratitude to my fabulous husband Michael and my incredible little girl Emma. My daughter's beautiful, bright light made the act of opening my kimono a joyful one, and she demonstrated endless patience when Mommy was busy writing. Michael, the Mighty Wielder of the Red Pen, gently yet relentlessly pursued the perfectly-edited manuscript, helping to transform a good book into a great one. He is a source of never-ending support, encouragement, and unconditional love; without him, *Opening the Kimono* would not exist. He is the macaroni to my cheese.

Finally, I humbly and graciously acknowledge Spirit for making all things possible. From the bottom of my most grateful heart, thank you, thank you, thank you for supplying me with the words and the courage to share them.

ABOUT THE AUTHOR

THERESA ROSE is a freelance writer, Reiki Master, intuitive healer, meditation facilitator and motivational speaker. Her mission is to educate, entertain, and inspire people to heal themselves, become aware of their unlimited power, and create their own unique, dogma-free relationship with Spirit. She holds a Bachelor of Arts degree in Business Management from Eckerd College and is a member of the Florida Writers Association and the Independent Book Publishers Association. Theresa lives in Sarasota, Florida with her husband Michael and her precocious little sprite Emma. For more information on Theresa's work, please visit www.theresarose.net.